X

D0872397

While Cannons Roared

The Civil War Behind the Lines

Also by John M. Taylor

Confederate Raider: Raphael Semmes of the Alabama

William Henry Seward: Lincoln's Right Hand

General Maxwell Taylor: The Sword and the Pen

Garfield of Ohio

From the White House Inkwell

Korea's Syngman Rhee
(writing as Richard C. Allen)

While Cannons Roared

The Civil War Behind the Lines

John M. Taylor

BRASSEY'S

Washington • London

Brassey's Editorial Offices: Brassey's Order Department:
22883 Quicksilver Drive   P.O. Box 960
Dulles, Virginia 20166   Herndon, Virginia 20172

Brassey's books are available at special discounts for bulk purchases for sales promotions, premiums, fund-raising, or educational use.

Library of Congress Cataloging-in-Publication Data

Taylor, John M. 1930–
    While cannons roared: the Civil War Behind the lines/
John M. Taylor. – 1st ed.
        p.   cm.
    Includes index.
    ISBN 1-57488-150-7 (hardcover)
    1. United States–History–Civil War, 1861–1865–Social aspects.
I. Title.
E468.9.T39   1997
973.7′1–dc21   97–27177
                                           CIP

Typeset by Page Graphics, Inc.

First Edition
10 9 8 7 6 5 4 3 2 1

Printed in the United States of America

For Alice, Kathy, and Jim

Contents

Preface

Winston Churchill called the American Civil War the noblest and least avoidable of the great wars up to that time. Whether it was in fact an "irrepressible conflict," as William H. Seward prophesied, it has certainly proved a boon to the publishing industry. Robert Cowley, editor of *Military History Quarterly*, speculates that as many as 50,000 books on Civil War subjects may have been published since 1865. This estimate does not include articles in scores of periodicals, some of which, like *Civil War Times Illustrated*, are devoted exclusively to the best-remembered and best-chronicled era in American history.

Although the most recent surge of interest in the Civil War owes much to Ken Burns's TV series, the war has never been out of the national consciousness. Mark Twain wrote in 1883 that the Civil War was, in the South, what A.D. is elsewhere: things are dated from it. The fact that it was the first American conflict in the era of photography makes it vivid even today. And on the eve of a new century, there are still many Americans whose great-grandfathers fought in the war, and whose recollections have passed down from generation to generation.

Certainly the war never lost its hold on the generation that lived through it, even noncombatants. Historian Henry Adams, who served in the American legation in London during the war, wondered "whether any of us will ever be able to live contented lives in times of peace and laziness. Our generation has been stirred up from its lowest layers, and there is that in its history which will stamp every member of it until we are all in our graves." Long after the war a Confederate veteran wrote,

> Who knows but it may be given to us, after this life, to meet again in the old quarters, to play chess and draughts, to get up soon to answer the morning roll call, to fall in at the tap of the drum for drill and dress parade, and again to hastily don our war gear . . . .

And after the battle, then the slain and wounded will arise, and all will meet together under the two flags, all sound and well, and there will be talking and laughter and cheers, and all will say: Did it not seem real? Was it not as in the old days?*

More than a century later, the war continues its hold on the popular imagination. Its issues were deep-seated and are still debated. What was the nature of the compact that bound the states into a federal union? Could any nation live, in Lincoln's term, half slave and half free? The United States would fight four major wars in the 20th century, but none—not even Vietnam—would affect the social fabric of the country as profoundly as did the Civil War.

In the narrow terms of military history, the Civil War was a watershed. For the first time, railroads played an essential role. The availability of repeating rifles made obsolete much of the military doctrine that had been preached since the time of Napoleon. Total war, as practiced by Sherman and others, was an ominous harbinger of the world wars of a later century.

Is there anything fresh to say about the Civil War period? Indeed there is. However important the war in terms of its issues and methodology, ultimately it was the story of thousands of people, caught up in forces they did not fully understand. To the soldier in the trenches, the most immediate issue was one of survival. Among the officers, war, however dangerous and unpleasant, offered prospects of glory. And the war introduced an element of passion even into the world of everyday politics.

The reader looking for detailed narratives of great battles will not find many in this book. Every engagement of the war worth chronicling—and quite a few that are not—has been adequately covered somewhere. Many of the stories in this volume are from "behind the lines," yet they are no less interesting on this account. How many readers are aware that President Lincoln paid a substitute to fight for him in 1864? How many know of the carelessness that led to the sinking of the famous *Monitor*? Although the circumstances of Lincoln's assassination are well known, only the most dedicated Civil War buffs are familiar with the assault on Secretary of State Seward and two other members of his family on the night Lincoln was shot.

Of the 21 chapters in this book, 15 have appeared in periodical form, the most frequent outlet having been *Civil War Times Illustrated*. The earliest of the articles appeared in 1978, the most recent in 1997. Of the remaining six, two have been adapted from my biographies of William H. Seward and Raphael Semmes and four are previously unpublished. In some of the articles I have included endnotes to indicate the source of quotations. For most of the chap-

---

*Bruce Catton, *Never Call Retreat* (New York: Doubleday, 1965), 456.

ters, however, my early drafts are long gone, and with them the detailed notes on sources.

All except three of the previously published chapters have been edited to varying degrees, proving once again that no article is ever truly "finished." In this polishing as in all matters relating to this book I am much indebted to my wife, Priscilla, editor of Phi Beta Kappa's quarterly *Key Reporter* and an associate editor of the *New York Public Library Writer's Guide to Style and Usage*, for her support and assistance.

John M. Taylor
McLean, Virginia
January 1997

While Cannons Roared

CHAPTER 1

"Compassion Is Always Due to an Enraged Imbecile"

O<small>N</small> A SUMMER DAY in 1855 the commanding general of the U.S. Army took pen in hand at his headquarters in New York City. Addressing his superior, the secretary of war, he enumerated numerous grievances, working his way up to a venomous close. "Notwithstanding the representations of your beneficiaries and sycophants that you are . . . entrenched in the favor of the President," he wrote, "I ask that this letter may be laid before [President Franklin Pierce]."

Upon receipt of the general's letter, the secretary of war was equal to the occasion. "Having early in this correspondence stamped you with falsehood," he replied, "I have ceased to regard your abuse, and . . . I am gratified to be relieved from the necessity of further exposing your malignity and depravity."

Although feuds were plentiful in the Old Army, the enmity between Winfield Scott and Jefferson Davis was something special. It was not merely professional rivalry, for the 70-year-old Scott was a military icon, a hero to the vast majority of his countrymen. The enmity between the general and his nominal superior was largely chemical, born of an instinctive dislike. While there were milestones along the way of the Scott-Davis feud, and even a rationale in terms of the Army chain of command, these do not tell the whole story. In the end it was a matter of personal incompatibility, one underscored by the fact that they represented different generations and different political parties.

Considering all this, it is interesting that the two protagonists shared a number of qualities. Both were Southerners, Scott being from Virginia, Davis from Mississippi. Each sprang from a middle-class background; each was patriotic and brave; and it should be noted, in view of Davis's subsequent career, that in the 1850s his loyalty to the Union was as unquestioned as Scott's. Unfortunately, the two men also shared a number of negative qualities: vanity, a preoccupation with protocol, and a devastating lack of anything resembling a sense of humor.

Although Davis is perhaps better remembered today, in 1855 he was little known by comparison with Winfield Scott. It was Scott who had provided the nation with some of its few moments of glory in the War of 1812, making his reputation at Chippewa and Lundy's Lane. In the decades that followed he symbolized the growing professionalism of American arms. Although not a West Pointer, he encouraged the development of the military academy as a means of lessening the country's dependence on militia. He deplored the extent of alcoholism in the Army, and became a courageous crusader for temperance.

Scott was not only one of the country's most respected soldiers, he was also one of the most flamboyant. Standing nearly 6 feet 5 inches tall, he prided himself on his own immaculate grooming and that of his staff. He rarely traveled without a retinue of aides, who were not above referring to their chief as "Old Fuss and Feathers." But there was more to Scott than pomp: He looked after his men. When, during the Black Hawk War, cholera broke out on a transport carrying his regiment, Scott himself nursed the sick, working day and night to alleviate their suffering.

It was the Mexican War that established Scott as the nation's foremost soldier. This was hardly President Polk's intention, for he was most reluctant to employ soldiers of a Whig orientation who might emerge from the war as political rivals. Nevertheless, when Zachary Taylor's campaign in northern Mexico failed to bring Santa Anna to his knees, Scott was authorized to lead an amphibious campaign aimed at Mexico City. It was Scott's remarkable campaign from Veracruz—the largest amphibious operation ever undertaken to that time—that led to the capture of Mexico City in September 1847.

The Scott-Davis feud had its genesis in the Mexican War. Their first skirmish related to arms for the regiment that Davis commanded in Mexico. The Mississippian was a West Pointer, as thirsty for glory as the young Scott had been. Davis was convinced of the merit of the new Whitney rifles and asked for his regiment to be equipped with them. Scott argued that the rifles had been insufficiently tested, and turned Davis down. In the end President Polk sided with Davis, and his judgment was vindicated when Davis's regiment served with distinction in Mexico.

During the war, Davis made an interesting request: that he be allowed to serve under Zachary Taylor for the remainder of the war. There was a poignancy to this request, because Davis had briefly been Taylor's son-in-law. Sarah Taylor had eloped with Davis in 1839, only to succumb to malaria after being married barely three months. For a time there had been total estrangement between Davis and Taylor, who had opposed the marriage. But somehow there was a reconciliation, and Davis's wartime request to

Gen. Winfield
Scott, in the 1850s
America's most
famous living
soldier.
Library of Congress

serve under Taylor was granted. He joined the camp of Scott's chief rival for
military glory.

After the war the protagonists went their separate ways: Taylor became
president, Davis was elected senator from Mississippi, and Scott became the
nation's first lieutenant general since George Washington. Scott was also a
candidate for president, but 1852 was not a Whig year. The Scott ticket was
overwhelmed at the polls, despite the relative obscurity of the Democratic
standard-bearer, Franklin Pierce.

In part because of Scott's political ambitions, it took his supporters in
Congress three years to enact the legislation promoting him to lieutenant
general. Still, on the last day of his term, President Millard Fillmore signed
the appropriations bill that included as one of its provisions promotion for
Scott. So strong was the feeling for and against the erstwhile presidential
candidate that his partisans took turns standing watch over the recording
clerks, lest the provision for Scott somehow be excluded from the final bill!
Not surprisingly, one of the more vociferous opponents to the bill promoting
Scott was the senator from Mississippi, Jefferson Davis.

With the inauguration of President Pierce, Scott had his promotion but he
had Davis as secretary of war. It did not take the general long to make his

feelings known. In a clear gesture of defiance, he packed up his Washington headquarters and moved it, bag and baggage, to New York City. From Scott's perspective this may have been a mistake. Orders affecting the army emanated from the War Department, and the War Department was in Washington. By his self-exile Scott left his rival in effective control of the administrative machinery.

Had Scott and Davis been required to transact army business face to face, their quarrel might have been resolved either by a limited accommodation or by the resignation of one protagonist. But this was not to be, and the uniquely bitter relationship between the commanding general and his secretary of war continued with a squabble over travel expenses. Scott traveled extensively on army business, and billed the department according to his mileage. To be sure, regulations provided for reimbursement only for travel "under written and special orders." But Scott acknowledged only one superior—the president—and the seemingly trivial matter of travel vouchers raised the issue of the commanding general's relationship to the secretary of war. A more tactful man than Jefferson Davis might have avoided a quarrel over travel vouchers, and reserved his ire for some matter of greater substance.

Jefferson Davis, at about the time of his service as Franklin Pierce's secretary of war. *Library of Congress*

But this was not his way, and in 1853 he infuriated Scott by supporting a War Department auditor who had questioned one of Scott's travel bills.

The general had his revenge, however, in an equally petty dispute, this time over pay. Scott interpreted his promotion as carrying with it the pay and perquisites of a lieutenant general, even though Congress had provided no additional funds. Davis was thus able to contend that Scott's new rank was entirely honorary. For much of 1855 angry letters flew between Washington and New York City. At length, in October, President Pierce referred the issue to his attorney general for resolution. When Attorney General Caleb Cushing upheld Scott, Davis briefly contemplated resignation before deciding against so drastic a step.

One may ask how the two antagonists found time for the performance of their official duties. Somehow they managed, and it was Davis who had much the greater influence on army policies. While Scott became a frequent visitor to West Point, an institution in which he took a paternal interest, Davis undertook a number of reforms on behalf of the peacetime army. Modern rifles replaced the smoothbores that dated back to the War of 1812; a new text on infantry tactics was introduced to replace one written, as luck would have it, by Winfield Scott. Davis even introduced camels to the American West, on the theory that if Napoleon could employ them in Egypt, they could be used on the American frontier. As secretary of war, Davis was ambitious, innovative, and effective, and there was no place in his scheme of things for a doddering old monument to past glory such as Winfield Scott.

To be sure, this view was not Davis's alone; the entire Pierce administration would have dearly loved to be rid of the officious Scott. It seemed somehow unfair that a political opponent, thoroughly trounced at the polls, should be an ex officio part of the administration. Meanwhile, Scott's hostility toward Pierce and Davis passed beyond matters of travel and protocol; he despised the slaveholder ruffians whom the government supported in Kansas, and was suspicious of the president's pro-Southern tilt in general.

Notwithstanding the banality of some of their disputes, the Scott-Davis clash raised fundamental questions about the relative positions of the commanding general and the secretary of war. Scott's view of his position was close to that of a French observer, Col. Camille Ferri Pisani, who wrote from Washington in 1861:

> The staff of the regular and permanent army of the United States comprises only one higher officer. General Scott occupies this post with the rank of Lieutenant General. The title gives him over-all command of the Army, both in peace and war. It is a kind of non-political ministry, especially concerned with military personnel and the movement of troops. The Minister of War, on the other hand, is more especially in charge of the administration.

However much Davis might dispute this interpretation, there was nothing in law to give him authority over Scott except the extent to which he might embody presidential authority. Scott maintained, in this connection, that he was not bound by an order from the secretary unless it stipulated, "By order of the President." In response, Davis turned once more to Attorney General Cushing, and this time the decision was more to his liking. Cushing ruled that orders from the secretary of war must be assumed to be those of the chief executive whether or not they included the magic words, "By order of the President."

The Pierce administration drifted to a close amid a crescendo of abuse between Scott and Davis. On one occasion Davis wrote the commanding general,

> Your petulance, characteristic egotism, and recklessness of accusa-
> tion have imposed on me the task of unveiling some of your defor-
> mities. To do this I have been compelled to draw upon some
> portions of your history not written by yourself. . . . It is sincerely
> to be hoped that those who follow you . . . will select for their imi-
> tation some other model than one whose military career has been
> marked by querulousness, insubordination, greed of lucre and
> want of truth.

Scott was equal to the occasion; in a letter of May 21, 1856, he philoso-
phized,

> My silence, under the new provocation, has been the result first of
> pity, and next, forgetfulness. Compassion is always due to an en-
> raged imbecile, who lays about him in blows which hurt only him-
> self, or who, at the worst, seeks to stifle his opponents by naughty
> words.

Clearly, Scott was not the easiest person in the world to get along with. And yet, considering his services to the nation, one is tempted to sympathize with the Old Warrior. As one author has noted, Davis was "coldly vain, where Scott was emotionally and impulsively vain." It is a fair distinction. Scott would have presented a challenge to any secretary of war, particularly given the ambiguities of the command relationship. Yet a bigger man than Davis would have made allowance for the older man's age and ego and would not have allowed their relations to degenerate to the level they did.

In time, Scott took up residence at Wormley's Hotel in Washington, his rooms filled with mementos of Chippewa, Cerro Gordo, and Chapultepec. He came to acknowledge his idiosyncrasies, remarking to visitors that at his age, compliments had become a necessity. When, in the first year of the Civil

War, he was displaced by the up-and-coming George B. McClellan—nearly 40 years his junior—Scott yielded gracefully and moved to West Point, where he passed his final years.

As for Davis, his tour as secretary of war stood him in good stead as president of an embattled Confederacy. Nevertheless, certain of the traits that had surfaced in his quarrel with Scott were reflected in his dealings with some of his wartime colleagues. Although Davis maintained a reasonable degree of harmony within his cabinet, his relations with a number of his generals came to be strained by his desire to oversee every aspect of the war effort. In particular, his running feuds with generals Joseph E. Johnston and P. G. T. Beauregard were damaging to the Confederate cause. Although the entire onus for these disputes cannot be laid on Davis, it is also true that his skills were not those of a conciliator. Whatever his office, Davis was certain of his own rectitude and determined to exercise every prerogative.

Scott eventually wrote a memoir that appeared in 1865. At a time when anything derogatory that he might say of Davis would have been cheered throughout the North, Scott virtually ignored him. By 1881, when Davis's memoir, *The Rise and Fall of the Confederate Government*, appeared, the author's peacetime feud with Winfield Scott had been overshadowed by his need to justify his role in a bloody civil war.

So it was that each protagonist, for reasons of his own, chose to ignore in his memoir the feud that had dominated the Franklin Pierce administration. Davis had more important actions to defend, while Scott chose silence as the ultimate rebuke

CHAPTER 2

"I Could Have
Surrendered Washington"

IT WAS AN AUTUMN for licking wounds. The previous July had seen the Federal disaster at Manassas, followed by calls for Gen. George B. McClellan to command the Army of the Potomac. Hopes for "Little Mac" were high, and even skeptics were impressed with the vigor he brought to the army's training and equipment. "He was seen in the camps or on the parade grounds every day," wrote historian Bruce Catton, "appearing in the morning and not disappearing until dark, seeing everything, being seen by everyone."

There were demands that McClellan do something with the fine army he had created, but these voices were as yet muted, and McClellan was not prepared for a major move. But some show of initiative was called for. In the months after Bull Run, the Confederates had occupied Leesburg, some 25 miles west of Washington, but the town was said to be lightly defended. On October 19, McClellan sent Brig. Gen. George McCall's division on a reconnaissance in the direction of Leesburg. At the same time, he ordered Brig. Gen. Charles P. Stone, who commanded a division on the Maryland side of the Potomac, to keep a sharp eye on the Virginia side, to see whether McCall's advance caused the Confederates to evacuate Leesburg. "Perhaps a slight demonstration on your part," McClellan wrote McCall, would have the effect to move them." These orders were notably vague, and the measures taken to implement them would lead to disaster.

In response to McClellan's desire for a "slight demonstration," Stone ordered the 1,700-man brigade commanded by Col. Edward D. Baker to cross the river near Leesburg and threaten the flank of the Confederate force facing McCall. Paradoxically, Baker was far better known outside the army than Stone was. The junior officer was a prominent politician and a friend of President Lincoln; he had been elected to the U.S. Senate from Oregon in 1860. When the war broke out, Baker resigned from the Senate, raised a

8

regiment of volunteers, and, in the fashion of the day, was elected its colonel. Like many volunteer officers, Baker was enthusiastic and brave but lacked experience in battle.

Baker led his regiment across the Potomac on October 21. The first elements had barely scaled Ball's Bluff on the Virginia side when they were attacked by a substantial Rebel force. Baker had only begun to make some dispositions to meet this threat when he was killed by a Confederate sharpshooter. His men attempted to return to their boats, but there were only three boats and the evacuation turned into a rout.

Of Baker's 1,700-man command, some 200 were killed and another 700 captured; among the wounded was one destined for later fame, justice-to-be Oliver Wendell Holmes Jr. Although the numbers involved were small compared with those at Manassas, the debacle at Ball's Bluff was one more shock to the North. Baker was eulogized as a hero and a martyr; responsibility for the defeat could not have been his. Who, then, was to blame?

Charles P. Stone, whose most conspicuous physical characteristic was a neat Vandyke goatee, was 37 years old at the time of Balls Bluff. A native of Greenfield, Massachusetts, he was the son of a respected local surgeon and civil leader. An 1845 graduate of West Point, he saw service in the Mexican War and remained in the army until 1856. Stone had an inquisitive mind. After leaving the army, he served on a commission to explore northern Mexico, and in 1860 published a monograph, *Notes on the State of Sonora*. But when civil war loomed, Stone volunteered his services to the army. He rejoined it as a colonel and was promptly made inspector general for the nation's capital—an innocuous-sounding title for a very sensitive position.

Stone's position was a critical one, for he was in effective control of the Washington, D.C., militia at a time when the city was virtually defenseless. His task was complicated by the fact that Washington was a "Southern" city, with strong secessionist sentiment. One of Stone's first actions in his new post was to hire detectives to help determine which militia companies could be relied upon. On one occasion when Stone complimented a company on its drill, the company commander remarked that he supposed he would soon be marching into Maryland "to keep the Yankees from coming down!"

Much of Stone's time was taken in looking to the safety of President Lincoln. Each night he would station a company of militia around the White House. Not surprisingly, Stone's energy and zeal made a good impression. Following Lincoln's inauguration, Stone was given command first of a brigade and then of a volunteer division, and promoted to brigadier general of volunteers. Then came Ball's Bluff.

Notwithstanding his solid record, Stone was politically vulnerable. He had made no secret of his Democratic political leanings or of the fact that, in

Gen. Charles P.
Stone, in a photo-
graph probably
taken in 1863.
Library of Congress

the faction-ridden Army of the Potomac, he was a supporter of the increasingly unpopular McClellan. And Stone campaigned as McClellan did: with
scrupulous regard for private property, enemy or otherwise. Did Stone carry
McClellan's practice a step too far? Historian Edward G. Longacre has told
how, while in Virginia, Stone "openly fraternized with local slave-owners,
liberally partaking of their hospitality. . . . Often he exchanged flags of truce
with Rebel officers and sent greetings to Confederates with whom he had
prior acquaintance."

    In all likelihood none of this would have gotten Stone into difficulty, even
after Ball's Bluff, had he not betrayed a certain disdain for civilian authority.
Like many of his army colleagues, Stone took the view that the war was
being fought solely to restore the Union, not to free the Negro. When runaway slaves entered his camp, Stone ordered them returned to their owners.
Word of this practice reached the governor of Massachusetts, John Andrew,
who rebuked Stone for employing soldiers from his state to return fugitive

slaves. Stone, in turn, told Governor Andrew to mind his own business. Whereupon the governor forwarded the relevant correspondence to Sen. Charles Sumner, who denounced Stone on the floor of the Senate. In a legal sense, Stone was right; it was not for a state governor to interfere with how Stone interpreted his orders. But their dispute coincided with the debacle at Ball's Bluff, and put Stone in the exposed position of a relatively junior officer with some very influential enemies.

Although Lincoln took no action at this time, Stone's enemies had the instrument with which to destroy him. In December 1861, Radicals in Congress had created a Joint Committee on the Conduct of the War. Its very name infringed upon the war-making responsibilities of the executive, but it was dominated by legislators whom Lincoln could not ignore. The committee, chaired by the gruff Ben Wade of Ohio, made Ball's Bluff its first order of business. Staffed largely with McClellan's enemies, the committee saw in Stone the archetypical lukewarm warrior represented by McClellan himself.

On January 5, 1862, Stone was called to testify before the committee. McClellan told him not to worry; he, McClellan, had informed the president of the facts regarding Ball's Bluff, and all Stone needed to worry about was taking care not to tell the committee anything of McClellan's plans. Stone thus appeared before the committee without any inkling of the very serious charges that were being framed—charges that impugned his very loyalty. He was taken aback by the obvious hostility of his questioners, but he gave his version of the battle of Ball's Bluff, placing most of the blame on the senators' late colleague, Edward Baker.

Stone confirmed that he had, on occasion, returned runaway slaves, but insisted that he had done this only when so ordered by civil authority. Altogether, it was a rather unpleasant session, but Stone left the Capitol convinced that he had acquitted himself well.

But there were other witnesses, and their testimony was unfriendly. Volunteer officers from his division spoke not only of Stone's conservative politics but of his rigid discipline and alleged bias against volunteers. There were reports, mostly hearsay, of contacts with Rebel sympathizers. After building up a record of testimony largely unfavorable to Stone, the committee passed its findings to Secretary of War Edwin M. Stanton, characterizing the testimony as tending "to impeach both the military capacity and the loyalty of General Stone." On January 28, Stanton ordered Stone's arrest.

McClellan was on the spot. On one hand, he was certain that the charges against Stone were unfounded; on the other hand, he recognized that the Wade committee could not be ignored and that his enemies were attempting to discredit him through Stone. McClellan temporized, asking whether Stone might be granted a second hearing. As a result, Stone appeared before the Wade committee again on January 31, though again without benefit of counsel and without knowledge of the charges against him.

Only when Wade informed him that there was evidence that "tends to prove that you have had undue communication with the enemy" did Stone fully appreciate his predicament. He asked to see the charges against him but his request was refused. He asked to cross-examine his accusers but this request, too, was denied. As he realized what was in store, Stone's reserve gave way to outrage:

> I thought there was one calumny that could not be brought against me. . . . I raised all the volunteer troops that were here during the seven dark days of last winter [when the capital was undefended]. . . . I could have surrendered Washington.

Stone's protest was in vain. Stanton was not disposed to antagonize the Radicals, and indicated that he found the testimony against Stone convincing. Once again he ordered McClellan to arrest Stone, and once again McClellan temporized. The first week of February, however, decided Stone's fate. A professed Unionist from Virginia came into Federal lines with the story that Stone had been on friendly terms with secessionists in his neighborhood. This testimony was no more substantial than earlier "evidence" of Stone's disloyalty, but it was more than McClellan was prepared to resist. He forwarded a summary of the refugee's story and advised Stanton that he would order Stone's arrest.

Stone was not without defenders. Retired general Winfield Scott, his superior in the first months of the war, was outraged by Stone's arrest, remarking that if he was a traitor, "we are all traitors." And what of President Lincoln? When Stanton advised him of Stone's arrest, the president seemed unable to focus on the issue. "I suppose you have good reasons for it," he told Stanton, "and having good reasons, I am glad I knew nothing of it until it was done." His reaction was defensive, and he must have realized that it was; he later commented that Stone's arrest came at a time when his son Willie was sick with the fever that would shortly take his life.

On Stanton's order, Stone was imprisoned first at Fort Lafayette in New York harbor and then at nearby Fort Hamilton. For almost two months he was in solitary confinement, but the conditions under which he was confined improved after his doctor testified that prison was undermining his health. But four more months passed, and Stone's repeated requests that he be either tried or released were ignored.

Fortunately, Stone had friends as well as enemies in Congress. Because the War Department's refusal to try him represented a violation of the Articles of War, Stone was released on August 16, 1862, as capriciously as he had been imprisoned. His release did not represent exoneration but was forced on the Lincoln administration by problems in assembling a court-martial in time of war. In reply to a Senate query, Lincoln wrote that Stone had not been tried "because in the state of military operations . . . the officers to constitute a court-martial . . . could not be withdrawn from duty without serious injury."

After his release Stone made the rounds of official Washington, attempting to find out who had been responsible for his arrest. In a display of buck-passing remarkable even for Washington, he met with contradiction on every hand. McClellan blamed Stanton, while Lincoln's chief of staff, Gen. Henry W. Halleck, put the onus on the president. Through the intervention of friends in Congress, however, Stone was granted a third opportunity to appear before the Wade committee.

This time, in February 1863, Stone was aware of the tenor of the testimony against him and able to deal with it. As a result, he was restored in rank and returned to active service. His requests for a court of inquiry, however, continued to be denied.

Back in the service, Stone served briefly as chief of staff to Gen. Nathaniel P. Banks in New Orleans during 1863. He subsequently returned east to command a brigade in the Army of the Potomac, but it was said that he was under constant surveillance. Early in 1864 he addressed a final appeal to Lincoln:

> This will be the last letter which I shall address to you during my life, or to justify myself in history. . . . I respectfully ask, for the sake of the service which I have loved and never dishonored . . . that some act, some word, some order, may issue from the executive which shall place my name clear above reproach, as I know it should be.

There was no reply, and in the autumn of 1864 Stone sent in his resignation.

Charles P. Stone, a trained engineer, had no difficulty in finding civil employment. After working for a mining company after the war, he accepted military service abroad as chief of staff of the Egyptian army. He served in Egypt for 13 years, returning to the United States in 1883. His last engineering project was in New York harbor, where he supervised construction of the base of the Statue of Liberty. He died in 1887, the last casualty of the battle of Ball's Bluff.

CHAPTER 3

Willard's of Washington

CHARLES DICKENS was not impressed. Writing in 1842 of his accommodations in Washington, the author told how

> The hotel in which we live is a long row of small houses, fronting on the street and opening at the back upon a common yard, in which hangs a great triangle. Whenever a servant is wanted, somebody beats on this triangle from one stroke up to seven, according to the number of the house in which his presence is required; and as all the servants are always being wanted . . . this enlivening engine is in full performance the whole day through.

Pre–Civil War Washington was not a mecca for travelers. Such hotels as it had were essentially seasonal boardinghouses—filled with tobacco-squirting politicians when Congress was in session, but operating far below capacity the remainder of the year. Discomfort was relative, however, and three hotels were widely regarded as the best of a bad lot. At the time of Dickens's visit the best-known establishments were Brown's Hotel, on the corner of Pennsylvania Avenue and West 6th Street; Gadsby's, across from Brown's; and Fuller's—where Dickens stayed—at the corner of 14th Street and Pennsylvania Avenue.

Banging triangles may have been an unnecessary irritant, but travelers in America had learned to live with many discomforts. Food was generally plentiful but unappetizing. Indoor plumbing was rare, and private baths were almost unheard of. Individual room keys had been introduced at the Tremont House in Boston, but were considered something of an innovation. The pervasive habit of chewing tobacco—a vice among American men—made for brown stains on the carpets of any hostelry.

But help was coming. Five years after Dickens's sojourn in Washington, the first of the Willard brothers came to town. Henry Augustus Willard, only 25 years of age, had been born in Vermont. He took a job as steward on a Hudson River steamboat, where he caught the eye of Benjamin Tayloe, one of the more prominent landowners in the nation's capital. Tayloe had long deplored the absence of a good hotel in Washington, and in 1847 he hired young Willard to run his string of boardinghouses on Pennsylvania Avenue. Two years later Willard was able to purchase the properties, and by 1853 he and his brother Joseph were proprietors of what was first called Willard's City Hotel.

Their establishment was by no means pretentious. Like most of its competitors, Willard's had not been designed as a hotel and was hardly distinguishable from any other row of townhouses. The brothers sought to give their establishment a personality. They purchased an adjacent church and turned it into a meeting hall. "Bathing rooms"—one for ladies, one for gentlemen—were installed on each floor. Servants were available to bring hot water.

The most impressive of the utility rooms was the great kitchen, which extended along the rear wall of the hotel. At busy times its multiple fireplaces were all in use, casting eerie shadows over an army of cooks and waiters who tended the spits. It was their food that the Willard brothers counted upon to give them a reputation. According to one account, Henry Willard "rose at three A.M. . . . and hied himself to market to select the finest fruits, vegetables, and meats for his guests." Catering as they were to the carriage trade, the Willards recognized the importance of public relations. At a time when Washington was dependent on wells for its water supply, the brothers hit upon a well that yielded some of the sweetest water in town. They sent a few barrels to the White House one day, and President James Buchanan was so impressed that Willard's became the purveyor of water for the Executive Mansion. Times were good. Henry Willard's son later recalled, "The years between 1853 and 1861 were years of prosperity for my father and his brother."

As Washington expanded westward, the Willard's convenience to the White House and the Treasury Department made it a favorite of politicians and foreign dignitaries. The Willard's dining room became known as the best in the city, and much of the business of government was allegedly transacted in its ornate lobby and bar.

In January 1861, with Lincoln the president-elect and seven Southern states out of the Union, Virginia initiated a conference aimed at heading off a war. Asked to host what became known as the Peace Conference, the Willard brothers were equal to the occasion; the conferees met for two weeks in Willard's Hall. The delegates were pleasantly surprised at the locale, and many booked their own rooms at the Willard.

164 ·   ILLUSTRATED NEWS.   [MARCH 12, 1853.

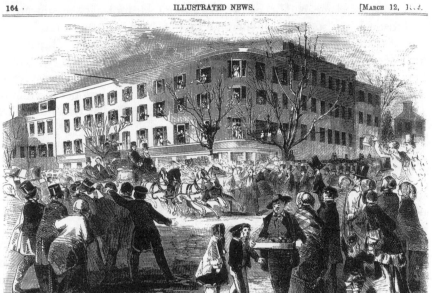

The Willard Hotel in 1853. *Leslie's Illustrated News*

Under the chairmanship of ex-president John Tyler, the peace delegates spent much of February in an eleventh-hour attempt to avert the "irrepressible conflict." In the end, they voted some compromise resolutions that had little influence North or South. But the delegates agreed that they had been handsomely treated by the brothers Willard.

The Civil War, more than any other event, conferred celebrity status on the Willard Hotel. It was there that president-elect Lincoln came on February 23, 1861, having traveled the last leg of his journey from Illinois in disguise because of the threat of assassination. To foil plotters, Lincoln slipped into the capital a day ahead of schedule, with the result that a businessman from New York was hastily evicted from parlor No. 6 to make room for the president-elect.

Nor was Lincoln's early arrival the only crisis. As the presidential party unpacked, it appeared that Mr. Lincoln's favorite slippers had been left behind. Henry Willard's son would recall,

> My father had [no slippers] large enough, for Mr. Lincoln had a very large foot. Nor did my father know of any slippers of adequate size in the hotel. He happened to think, however, of a pair of slippers belonging to my great grandfather . . . who was a guest of my parents at their private home across the street. . . . My great

grandfather was most delighted to lend his slippers to such a distinguished personage . . . and, as he had a good large foot, the slippers were found to fit Mr. Lincoln well.

According to the hotel ledger, the Lincoln party was charged $2.75 per room for a multiroom suite and three meals a day. Among additional items billed to the president-elect were $50 for champagne, $8 for brandy and whiskey, and a total of $100 for room service. White House credit was good, and Lincoln did not pay his bill until six weeks after his inauguration.

That summer the first battle of Manassas sent the Federal army reeling back on Washington, and a by-product of the defeat was considerable reeling at the Willard. The hotel had become such a watering spot for Federal officers that an outraged Walt Whitman brought it into one of his poems:

There you are, shoulder straps, but where are your companies? Where are your men?

Speak, blow, put on airs in Willard's sumptuous bar, or anywhere!

No explanation will save you. Bull Run is your work!

Whitman's verse was not the hotel's only brush with literature in these stirring times. A group of Bostonians, riding back to town from one of McClellan's reviews, passed the time with choruses of a soldier's song known as "John Brown's Body." One of the party, Julia Ward Howe, thought the words might be improved upon. Early the next morning, she awoke in her room at Willard's. She jumped out of bed, and with the stump of a pencil scrawled in the semidarkness the stanzas of "The Battle Hymn of the Republic."

As 1863 turned into 1864, the nation's capital manifested all the aspects of a boomtown. The population, exclusive of soldiers, had risen from 73,000 in 1860 to about 350,000. Telegraph wires were everywhere, connecting the War Department with the Capitol, the Navy Yard, and outlying encampments. Every hotel and every boardinghouse was filled—with contractors, clerks, embalmers, petty thieves, and just plain cranks. The streets rang with the clatter of army wagons and the oaths of their drivers. A sense of disorder was everywhere.

By 1864, prostitution vied with government service as the town's leading industry. Anyone venturing onto Pennsylvania Avenue was treated to the sight of gaudy courtesans parading with officers or sharing their carriages. The *Washington Star* claimed to have examined the statistics on prostitutes and concluded that the figure of 15,000 was too high. The actual total, the *Star* wrote, was closer to 5,000, up from 350 before the war.

Thus, the Willard was a bastion of privilege in a city that was experiencing the popular excesses endemic to wartime. As the war went on, capital society devoted itself increasingly to rounds of balls, receptions, theatricals, and benefits. Queen of Washington society was Kate Chase Sprague, the vivacious, newly married daughter of Lincoln's secretary of the treasury. The son of another cabinet member, Frederick Seward, wrote in 1863, "A year ago [Secretary Seward] was 'heartless' or 'unpatriotic' because he gave dinners; now the only complaint of him is that he don't have dancing."

Indeed, the war did little to inhibit conspicuous consumption. Guests at the Willard could begin their day with a breakfast that included such delicacies as fried oysters, steak, blancmange, and pâté. An equally gargantuan midday meal was followed by dinner at five o'clock, a robust tea at 7:30, and, finally, supper at around nine. Visitors from Britain—no dainty eaters themselves—were amazed at the quantity of food consumed by their American hosts.

In the midst of a stalemated war, the capital took time out to wonder at the midget "General" Tom Thumb and his bride on their honeymoon. They stayed at the Willard, of course, where at a dance in their honor General Thumb was resplendent in a black suit, patent leather boots, white kid gloves, and a necktie complete with breastpin. Mrs. Thumb wore a white satin gown decorated with green leaves and carnation buds.

Fire was a constant threat to any 19th-century hotel, and the danger was heightened by Washington's deserved reputation as a city of smokers and drinkers. A famous Union regiment, the Fire Zouaves, helped put out one fire at the Willard, but lesser blazes were all too frequent.

By the end of the war the Willard brothers were rich. They were also weary of the hotel business. They leased their famous hotel to the first of a series of management firms and went their separate ways. Henry continued to live in Washington, where he was active in civic affairs. His brother Joseph also lived in the capital, but after the death of his wife in 1871 he became something of a recluse.

Joseph Willard died in 1897, his brother in 1909. Majority interest in the hotel passed to Joseph's son, who was interested in building a new hotel on the site of the old. By the close of the century, competition in the hotel business was keen, and the jerry-built Willard, with its straggling roofline and creaking halls, seemed something of a relic.

Construction of the new Willard began early in 1901. The new edifice—designed by H. J. Hardenburg, the architect for New York's Plaza—was 12 stories high and boasted the capital's largest ballroom. On October 15, 1901, the *Washington Post* announced, "Another Washington hotel, acknowledged to be the most modern and lavishly equipped of them all, will open its doors to the public this evening at six o'clock."

Although the new hotel prospered, there were warning signs even then. The city's expansion was largely to the northwest, where luxury hotels such as the Shoreham and the Wardman Park came to challenge the new Willard.

The advent of the automobile, moreover, tended to neutralize the Willard's proximity to government offices in downtown Washington.

But the Willard of the 1920s was still a thing of splendor. Its arcade, which ran the length of the building from Pennsylvania Avenue to F Street, came to be known as Peacock Alley, not only for its floral decorations but for the extravagantly dressed promenaders who came to see and to be seen. It was at the tobacco shop at the Willard that Vice President Thomas Marshall summarized the state of the Union with his much-quoted remark, "What this country needs is a good five-cent cigar." The Willard, which boasted that it had hosted every American president since Millard Fillmore, had a final hour in the limelight when Calvin Coolidge made it a temporary White House for the first month of his presidency, following the death of President Harding.

The decades that followed brought severe problems to most downtown hotels: crime, inadequate transit, urban blight. The Willard's proximity to tourist spots delayed its demise, but on July 15, 1968, the hotel closed its doors. The few remaining tenants were unceremoniously evicted, and for years the boarded-up Willard was a monument to America's decaying cities.

Then the Willard took a turn for the better. The Pennsylvania Avenue Development Corporation, chartered by Congress to oversee the restoration of Pennsylvania Avenue and its environs, financed a rehabilitation of the Willard and its conversion into a combination hotel and office complex. The result was a structure whose turn-of-the-century Edwardian elegance would have flabbergasted the Willard brothers. Nevertheless, Charles Dickens would surely have wished the new hotel well.

CHAPTER 4

Lieutenant Grant and the Missing Money

LIEUTENANT GRANT was homesick. The war with Mexico was over, but the occupation lingered on. "Sam" Grant—no one called him by his given name, Ulysses—had not thought much of the Mexican War in the first place. Many years later he would call it one of the must unjust of wars, but as a professional Army officer he had done his duty. He had served with the armies of both Zachary Taylor and Winfield Scott. He had seen active service with the 4th Infantry Regiment, and had been brevetted for gallantry at Monterey.

The 25-year-old Grant, however, had never been seduced by the glory of war. Moreover, he was desperately lonesome for his fiancée, Julia Dent, to whom he had become engaged just before leaving for Mexico. On New Year's Day, 1848, Grant wrote from his camp near Mexico City, "It is now strongly believed that peace will be established before many months. I hope it may be so, for it is scarcely supportable for me to be separated from you so long, my Dearest Julia."

Grant's friend James Longstreet stopped by to say farewell; his unit had been ordered home. But the 4th Regiment had no orders, and Grant stayed on, his billet being that of regimental quartermaster. Grant had no special aptitude for administration, but he brought a certain initiative to his duties. When regimental funds were low, Grant organized a bakery, which not only provided bread for the regiment but sold its wares to the chief commissary at a profit.

One of Grant's responsibilities as quartermaster was the safekeeping of government funds, and this responsibility would prove his undoing. In June 1848, as the 4th Regiment finally prepared to go home, Grant became concerned about the safety of $1,000 in regiment funds—mostly in silver dollars—in his custody. He had no safe and the lock on his trunk was broken. He asked a fellow officer, Capt. John Gore, for permission to put the money sack in Gore's trunk, which had a strong lock. Gore was not enthusiastic, but it was hard to say no, and Gore acceded to Grant's request.

Gore affirmed later that he personally guarded the trunk during the day it was in his care, and kept it in his tent at night. The money was still in the trunk on June 12, when the 4th Regiment, part of the division commanded by Gen. William J. Worth, participated in flag-lowering ceremonies in Mexico City. Four nights later, however, on the road to Jalapa, the trunk was stolen from the tent occupied by Gore and another officer.

As Gore reconstructed the theft, the thieves carried the trunk some 600 yards to a millrace, broke it open, removed the money, and threw the trunk into a stream. A search of the stream on the morning of June 17 revealed, in Gore's words, "many small articles, but no money."

Although the trunk was Gore's, responsibility for the money was Grant's; transfer of physical custody had not altered the hard fact that Grant was responsible for all funds committed to his care. Probably on the advice of colleagues, Grant promptly requested a board of inquiry, and Worth convened one on June 25. Its findings provided both good news and bad.

On one hand, the board found that "no blame can attach to Lt. U.S. Grant, that he took every means to secure the Money . . . and they exonerate him from all censure." On the other hand, the board's findings in no way altered the fact that Grant was accountable for the missing funds, which were roughly equivalent to one year's pay for a second lieutenant.

Anyone who has ever taken on the IRS in a tax matter can sympathize with Grant's position. Indeed, IRS procedures, with their established channels for appeal, seem positively enlightened by comparison with the unresponsive bureaucracy that confronted Grant. So hopeless was any appeal through the army or the Treasury Department—the findings of the board of inquiry notwithstanding—that Grant did not even bother.

From time to time, friends sought to discover whether Grant could be helped in some way. A letter from a Treasury Department auditor in 1852, in response to a query, noted that Grant's file contained no appeal for relief; the auditor added cheerfully that, in any case, the rule governing such appeals was "to disallow them, having no discretion to do otherwise." Grant's only hope was to find a sponsor for a private relief bill.

The debt from this misadventure in Mexico was the first in a series of setbacks that were to dog Grant for more than a decade. The peacetime army proved to be a succession of dreary frontier postings. Promotion was slow. Grant failed at several business ventures while still in uniform, and gained a reputation as a drinker.

Grant was devoted to his wife, Julia, and when he was sent without her to an isolated post at Humboldt Bay, California, his drinking contributed to a falling out with his commanding officer. The upshot was that Grant resigned from the army in 1854, still liable for the money lost in Mexico. Although the government does not appear to have pressed for payment, Grant had no luck in getting relief through Congress. The first private bill on his behalf failed to pass in 1849. A similar bill was introduced in the next Congress by Rep. Jonathan Morris of Ohio, but appears not to have been reported out of committee.

All of this weighed upon Grant; in 1852 he wrote Julia of his concern at not being able to travel to Washington to plead his case once more. "If I cannot go," he wrote, "I want father to write to our members of Congress and have one set of my papers, on the subject of the stolen money. . . . It is very important that they should not be lost."

A week later, in another letter to Julia, he was more cheerful:

> I send you Capt. Calender's note by this letter. He has paid my tailor's bill so that I have not got a debt against me except my public debt, and that I shall go to Washington on Wednesday to try to have settled. I met [Edward] Marshall, member of Congress from California, who I knew very well in Mexico, and he promises to take the matter up as soon as he goes back to Washington.

If Marshall introduced yet another bill on Grant's behalf it did not pass. One can only speculate as to how the matter might have ended had the Civil War not intervened, for by 1861 Grant had been reduced to clerking in a leather goods store and was probably less capable of finding $1,000 than he had been 13 years before.

In 1861, however, Grant began the meteoric rise that led to his becoming the commanding general of the army and, later, president of the United States. A way station in Grant's redemption was his capture of Fort Donelson in February 1862. To the Confederate request for an armistice, Grant had replied that no terms except unconditional surrender could be accepted. "Unconditional Surrender Grant" became a hero throughout the North.

Soon he would not have to worry about the money lost in Mexico. A month after Fort Donelson fell, Rep. William A. Richardson of Illinois introduced "An Act for the Relief of Lt. Ulysses S. Grant." It was reported out favorably by the Committee on Military Affairs in April 1862 and passed by Congress on June 17. One thousand dollars must have seemed a small price for a major Rebel fort!

In his memoir Grant makes no mention of this painful episode, and who can blame him? Certain of his admirers, however, have sounded a defensive note in connection with Grant's 13-year indebtedness. William C. Church, in a biography published in 1926, even embellished the facts a bit, writing, "Though he was not responsible for the loss, Grant, when he was able to do so, made it good to the Treasury."

Ulysses S. Grant as
a brevet second
lieutenant in the
4th Infantry
Regiment.
*U.S. Military
Academy Library*

Not so. But today it seems no more than fair that this service-incurred debt, which hung over Grant so long, should finally have been resolved in his favor.

CHAPTER 5

Lincoln and Seward: A Washington Friendship

WHEN WILLIAM HENRY SEWARD entered the United States Senate in 1849, Horace Greeley wrote in the *New York Tribune* that "probably no man ever appeared for the first time in Congress so widely known and so warmly appreciated."[1] Ten years later the editor of the influential *Nation*, Edwin Godkin, wrote that the senator from New York was "perhaps the greatest constitutional lawyer in America, the clearest-headed statesman, a powerful and above all a most logical orator, and of all the public men of this country perhaps the least of a demagogue and the most of a gentleman."[2] In Washington it was said of Seward that he destroyed his enemies by making them his friends.

The object of this admiration was not your prototype statue in the park. At the outset of the Civil War, Seward was a white-haired 60-year-old, frail and slightly stooped. In an era when men favored beards and virile physiques, Seward's most prominent feature was his nose, which gave him the aspect of a jocular bird. Young Henry Adams remarked on the senator's "unorderly hair and clothes; hoarse voice; offhand manner; free talk, and perpetual cigar."[3] Adams felt an urge to color his hair some flaming tropical color.

In the spring of 1860 Seward had suffered what might have been a terminal political setback when the young Republican Party, scenting victory, passed over him in favor of Abraham Lincoln as its presidential nominee. Following the Republican victory, it had been widely assumed that Seward would occupy a prominent position in the new administration, and Lincoln had indeed offered the New Yorker the most prestigious post in his cabinet, that of secretary of state. North of the Mason-Dixon line the appointment was applauded. The senator was a two-time governor of his state, where he had been an early champion of penal reform and immigrant rights. Later, in the Senate, he had emerged as a leading spokesman for the antislavery movement—not a flaming abolitionist of the Charles Sumner mode, but an

24

William Henry
Seward, whom
Henry Adams
likened to "a wise
macaw," as
secretary of state.
Library of Congress

opponent of any extension of slavery, a group whose numbers included Abraham Lincoln. In 1858 Seward had delivered a widely publicized speech in which he called the struggle against slavery "an irrepressible conflict"— words that would come back to haunt him when the Republican Party sought a safe, noncontroversial candidate to run for president in 1860.

Although Lincoln and Seward had met occasionally in the 1850s, their real relationship began with Lincoln's inauguration in 1861. Lincoln, who once said that he had never willingly planted a thorn in any man's bosom, had planted one in Seward by defeating him for the presidential nomination. The new secretary of state was eight years older than Lincoln, better educated and far better traveled, and he boasted a record of public service that made Lincoln's single term in Congress seem paltry. Seward's friends made no secret of their belief that the secretary of state would be the dominant figure in the new administration, and their view was supported by the early rapport between Lincoln and his erstwhile rival. In the first month of the new administration Seward told his wife of a long carriage ride he had taken with the president, adding, "He is very cordial and kind toward me—simple, natural and agreeable."[4]

Seward was one of a few people to whom Lincoln showed an advance copy of his inaugural address, and the older man had a number of suggestions. He urged softer language in reference to the South and the addition of a conciliatory note at the close. Seward drafted an insert along these lines, but Lincoln preferred his own text. The result was that memorable passage beginning, "I am loath to close. We are not enemies but friends. . . ." The occasionally acerbic New Yorker was impressed; perhaps there was more to the "prairie statesman" than Seward had realized. He remarked to Charles Francis Adams that the president had "a curious vein of sentiment running through his thoughts which is his most valuable mental attribute."[5]

Seward attempted to keep an open mind about his chief, but there were frustrations. The new president seemed to lack plans for coping with the imminent dissolution of the Union. While Lincoln pondered, Seward—with his network of contacts in the capital—sought to nourish what he saw as latent Unionist sentiment in the South and in the border states. At the same time, he attempted to assure the visiting Confederate commissioners, who considered Seward the spokesman for the new administration, that Lincoln would do nothing rash in regard to beleaguered Fort Sumter.

These negotiations probably inspired the most controversial document of Seward's career, a memo he titled "Some Thoughts for the President's Consideration." The paper, dated April 1, 1861, began with the observation that the Lincoln administration, after a month in office, was still "without a policy, either domestic or foreign." To a considerable extent this was true; Lincoln's public pronouncements had been notably bland, and his cabinet was divided on the key issue of provisioning Fort Sumter. Seward, taking the initiative, suggested that the question before the public should be shifted from *slavery* to *disunion.* In other words, Seward argued, change the main issue "from what would be regarded as a party question, to one of patriotism."

In foreign policy, Seward invoked the Monroe Doctrine. Spain had just annexed Santo Domingo (today's Dominican Republic) and by arrangement with France was about to take over Haiti as well. Seward suggested that the administration demand explanations from Spain and France and, if satisfactory explanations were not forthcoming, "convene Congress and declare war against them." Seward was convinced, despite growing evidence to the contrary, that a foreign crisis would unite the country and nip secession in the bud. For one whose judgment was usually sound, Seward appears to have accepted rather uncritically some vague reports of latent Unionist sentiment in the South.

As if Seward's casual advocacy of a foreign war were not enough, the secretary closed with a proposal that future generations would consider heretical. Whatever policies were adopted, Seward wrote, must be pursued energetically. Either the president or "some member of his Cabinet" must take the lead. Closing his letter to Lincoln, the normally forthright Seward struck a disingenuous note, writing, "I neither seek to evade nor assume responsibility."[6]

Seward's presumptuousness has been roundly denounced by historians weaned on the Lincoln legend. It is worth recalling, therefore, that as of April 1861 Lincoln had shown no signs of greatness, and in fact appeared as vacillating as his predecessor, Buchanan. Moreover, in earlier administrations the secretary of state had often been the "premier," with responsibilities well beyond the conduct of diplomacy. The dominant figures in the Fillmore and Pierce administrations had been Secretary of State Daniel Webster and Secretary of War Jefferson Davis, respectively. Key cabinet officers were far more influential in the mid-19th century than any time since.

Nevertheless, Seward's "Thoughts" represented a crisis in terms of Seward's relations with Lincoln. The older man was confident that Lincoln would not allow him to leave the cabinet, but if he anticipated some form of capitulation on the part of the president he was badly mistaken. Lincoln replied on the same day that he received Seward's memorandum, defending his caution to date and ignoring Seward's more bellicose proposals. Whatever must be done, Lincoln wrote, "I must do." And in dealing with the issues Seward had raised, Lincoln would consult not only with the secretary of state but with the entire cabinet.

With the exchange of April 1 the relationship between Lincoln and Seward entered a new phase. For all his hints of resignation, the fate he feared most was exile to his home in upstate New York in a time of national crisis. Now, Seward was heard to remark that "old as he was, he had learned a lesson from this affair, and that was [that] he had better attend to his own business."[7] With their official relationship now clear, Lincoln and Seward moved into a period of the closest collaboration. The following month Seward wrote to his wife, Frances, that Lincoln's "magnanimity is almost superhuman. His confidence and sympathy increase every day."[8]

Seward's areas of responsibility within the new administration soon went far beyond those of later secretaries of state. Because he was a long-time friend of Gen. Winfield Scott, Seward often dealt on Lincoln's behalf with the venerable commanding general. He had a major voice in the distribution of offices in the key state of New York, although Lincoln, of course, had the final say. In 1861 and 1862, the State Department had major responsibilities for internal security. Seward was responsible for placing more than a thousand Rebel suspects—including the notorious spy, Rose Greenhow—in preventive detention. Censorship of the mails and the telegraph fell to Seward's department.

One morning, an old navy friend, John F. Winslow, called on Seward, bringing with him a representative of the Swedish American inventor, John Ericsson. The two visitors reported that Ericsson was in a position to build a counterpart to the ironclad warship said to be under construction in the South, but that the Navy Board was reluctant even to give it a trial. Seward introduced the two to Lincoln, and the next day accompanied them to the Navy Department. The navy was persuaded to underwrite Ericsson's experiment, and the result was the famous *Monitor*.

In the diplomatic arena, Seward gained presidential approval for his key diplomatic appointments, including those of Charles Francis Adams to London and William Dayton to Paris. He began a series of dispatches to American representatives abroad, keeping them advised on the military situation and providing talking points for their dealings with host governments. At the end of 1861 Seward demonstrated his usual sound judgment at the time of the *Trent* incident, when the U.S. seizure of a British packet, and the capture of two Confederate officials on board, threatened war with Britain. Seward counseled restraint, and ultimately was able to persuade Lincoln and a majority of the cabinet that the Confederate commissioners must be returned to British protection.

Lincoln's cabinet was an unusual combination of ability and mediocrity. Drawn as it was from two competing parties—the northern Whigs and the northern Democrats—it also had more than its share of built-in animosities. Seward quickly became a focus of controversy, in part because of the president's clear reliance on him. Several department heads complained about the infrequency of cabinet meetings and about Seward's perceived influence over the president. Most suspicious of all was navy secretary Gideon Welles, an erstwhile Connecticut Democrat who left his fulminations for posterity in his diary.

When Seward accepted his portfolio as secretary of state, he had bought a new house, known as the Old Clubhouse, across Pennsylvania Avenue on the corner of Lafayette Park. By the autumn of 1861 Lincoln had fallen into the habit of dropping in at Seward's home unannounced. There Lincoln could escape the ever-present office seekers, and Seward the termagant Mary Lincoln, who periodically denounced him as "that dirty abolitionist sneak." The two men took carriage rides together, and their mutual respect gradually grew into friendship. On important matters the two had much in common. Both were conservatives by instinct, though Seward liked nothing more than to float propositions that were likely to generate opposition. On the key issue of race, their views were similar. Both saw blacks as inferior to whites in capability, but were convinced that blacks, too, had a right to freedom and the pursuit of happiness. Both had misgivings about giving blacks the vote, but wished to keep all options open.

Although Seward, unlike Lincoln, had been brought up in affluence, the law was a common bond. So too was a keen sense of humor, and the ease with which the two swapped stories was infuriating to outsiders like secretaries Chase and Welles. Both Seward and Lincoln tended to be careless in matters of dress, and impatient with protocol. But there were differences, too. Both were astute judges of human nature, but Lincoln was clearly the master. Whatever the differences in their formal education, Lincoln was by far the better writer. Once when Seward preferred his own language to some changes that Lincoln had made in a letter to the British prime minister, Lord Palmerston, the cabinet was treated to a good-natured exchange:

> "Mr. Secretary, do you suppose Palmerston will understand our position from my letter, just as it is?"

> "Certainly, Mr. President."

> "Do you suppose the London *Times* will?"

> "Certainly."

> "Do you suppose the average Englishman of affairs will?"

> "Certainly. It cannot be mistaken in England."

> "Do you suppose that a hackman on his box will understand it?"

> "Very readily, Mr. President."

> "Very well, Mr. Secretary, I guess we'll let her slide just as she is."[9]

It was a measure of their closeness that Lincoln was not above making Seward the butt of his humor. The president did not care for profanity, and on a ride out to visit the Army of the Potomac he was annoyed by a stream of oaths from his carriage driver. Lincoln tapped him on the shoulder and asked,

> "Excuse me, my friend, are you an Episcopalian?"

> "No, Mr. President," replied the man. "I am a Methodist."

> "Well," said Lincoln, "I thought you must be an Episcopalian, because you swear just like Governor Seward, who is a church warden."[10]

For much of 1862 Lincoln wrestled with the possibility of emancipating slaves in the seceded states as a military measure. He moved with characteristic deliberation, however, and many of those who opposed his cautious approach were inclined to place the blame on Seward. Anti-Seward sentiment was fanned by Secretary of the Treasury Salmon P. Chase, who regarded himself as the ablest and wisest of Lincoln's cabinet and resented the fact that his advice was not more frequently sought. Ambitious for the presidential nomination in 1864, Chase sought to ingratiate himself with the radical Republicans in Congress. He lent a sympathetic ear to complaints about Seward's excessive influence on Lincoln, and probably fanned them.

Three days after the Federal military debacle at Fredericksburg, in December 1862, Republican senators held two heated caucuses in which Seward was openly denounced. Cooler heads sidetracked a resolution that attacked Seward by name, but the conferees agreed to demand that Lincoln reorganize his cabinet, and they chose a committee of nine to present their grievances to the president. On the evening of December 18 the committee met with Lincoln for three hours. They charged Seward with being only mildly opposed to slavery and with exercising undue influence on administration policy. They demanded that cabinet meetings be held more frequently, and by implication urged a larger voice for Chase. Lincoln, recognizing that he had a crisis on his hands, asked the senators to return the following night.

Seward, on hearing about the earlier caucus, submitted his resignation to relieve Lincoln of any embarrassment. After meeting with the senators, Lincoln walked across Lafayette Park for a talk with Seward. The secretary was feeling sorry for himself, but all the while insisted that retirement would be a relief. "Ah, yes, Governor," Lincoln observed, "That will do very well for you, but . . . I can't get out."[11]

The result was one of Lincoln's political triumphs. He first called the cabinet together, without Seward, and expressed concern about any disruption of his official family. He suggested that Seward was being unfairly blamed for unpopular administration policies, and asked that the cabinet join him in meeting with the senatorial committee that evening.

When the senators returned to the White House, they were surprised to find themselves in the presence of the entire cabinet except for Seward. The president launched a defense of his administration. He defended the relative infrequency of cabinet meetings, noting that the cabinet was in agreement on major policy matters and that Seward made no important decisions without his, Lincoln's, consent. Chase was severely embarrassed, for he could not deny the basic truth of what Lincoln had said without being contradicted by his cabinet colleagues. Reluctantly, Chase acknowledged that the cabinet was harmonious. After a marathon five-hour session, Lincoln asked the eight senators present if they still thought Seward should be replaced. Only four voted in the affirmative.

Chase, badly outmaneuvered, submitted his resignation the following day. Lincoln seized the paper with alacrity, but he no more intended to accept it than he had intended to accept Seward's. He wanted to keep both Seward and Chase at their posts, so that his cabinet might be perceived as including all factions. Gideon Welles, who had reluctantly supported Seward against the radical senators, wrote in his diary, "Seward comforts [Lincoln]; Chase he deems a necessity."[12]

With this confrontation behind him, it was a grateful secretary of state who returned to his diplomatic duties at the turn of the year. Federal military prospects were still bleak, but the period of greatest danger for European recognition of the Confederacy had passed. In February 1863 the Lincoln administration refused an offer by France to mediate the American conflict. The United States won a diplomatic victory in September 1863 when Britain prevented the departure of two powerful warships that had been destined for the Confederacy. Seward's immediate concern then became the cruisers that were being constructed in France for the Confederacy. These, too, were kept out of hostile hands.

But there were also setbacks. While the Union navy sought desperately to capture a Confederate blockade runner, the *Nashville*, the president and his secretary of state had a private bet on the outcome. Not for the first time, Seward proved too optimistic. The collector for New York, Hiram Barney, wired Lincoln, "You have won the quart of hazelnuts from the Secretary of State. The *Nashville* is not destroyed but is actively at work."[13]

Although Seward's stock within the Republican Party was on the decline, there were those who wanted him to try again for the party's presidential nomination. No president since Andrew Jackson had served two terms, and it was not necessary to be anti-Lincoln to support Seward for the 1864 nomination. The secretary, however, would have no part of it. At his direction, sixteen "Seward Clubs" that had been established in Pennsylvania changed their name to "Republican." Seward told visitors that he had abandoned party considerations for the duration, and he ignored suggestions that he run again for the Senate.

As the military tide turned in 1864, Seward's task eased into a routine. Journalist Noah Brooks recalled a reception at the Seward residence:

> The Secretary of State does not keep great state at his residence, though his upstairs parlors were quite tastefully furnished—marble busts, engravings, flowers and paintings being the most noticeable objects in the room, unless it was the prodigious nose of Seward. He advanced from the rear of the parlors as a batch of names was called, shaking hands with . . . his matchless *suaviter in modo* as each caller was presented.[14]

On April 2, 1865, Lee evacuated Richmond; the war's end was clearly in sight. Three days later, as Seward was riding in his carriage along Vermont Avenue, the coach was halted to repair a balky door. The horses bolted, and because the driver had been left behind, Seward attempted to gather the reins himself and bring things under control. Alas, the 64-year-old Seward was thrown onto the street, breaking his jaw, dislocating a shoulder, and breaking his right arm. His recovery was slow and painful.

On the night of Lincoln's assassination, as Seward lay half asleep in an upstairs bedroom in his residence, he was attacked and almost killed by one of John Wilkes Booth's henchmen, employing a Bowie knife. Lewis Paine inflicted no fewer than seven stab wounds on the secretary before making his escape. At first it was feared that Seward's wounds were fatal, but his usual resilience asserted itself.*

Although Seward enjoyed the exercise of power, he was prone to view his own career with a degree of fatalism. It seemed especially ironic now that, even as he himself escaped death, his family did not. Frances Seward, who was far more liberal in her politics than her husband, died only weeks after her husband survived the assassin's knife. Their one daughter, Fanny, long afflicted with tuberculosis, succumbed in October of the same year.

Seward continued as secretary of state in the Andrew Johnson administration, writing many of the president's key veto messages and pressing successfully for the famous Alaska purchase. He welcomed back to Washington many of those Southerners with whom he had exchanged hospitality before the war. One day, on the street, he encountered Robert Hunter, an erstwhile member of the Confederate cabinet who had earlier served with Seward in the Senate. Seward invited him to dinner that evening, and the two talked of old times. Hunter was puzzled to see a paper sticking out from under his dinner plate. When he examined the paper it turned out to be a pardon—in all likelihood the reason for his trip to Washington.

Seward would never emerge from under the shadow of Abraham Lincoln. After Seward's death in 1872, Charles Francis Adams delivered a eulogy in which he gave much of the credit for the Lincoln administration's successes to the man from New York. In a remarkable riposte, Seward's long-time antagonist, Gideon Welles, published a small book devoted entirely to refuting Adams's eulogy. Even Welles, however, conceded that "if [Seward] had not the will which is necessary for a chief, he had the sustaining qualities which are valuable in serving a capable leader."[15]

American history affords few more complex figures than William Henry Seward. As a person he was a model not only of rectitude but of warmth and charm. Although proud of his own achievements, he was easy and unaffected with others, treating servants and messengers with the some consideration that he showed foreign envoys. When defeated for the presidency by someone he considered less qualified than himself, he became not only a trusted subordinate but a devoted friend. Small wonder that Lincoln called him "a man without gall."[16]

---

*The assassination attempt is discussed further in Chapter 17.

CHAPTER 6

"You Are the Enemy
of Our Set"

GEN. GEORGE G. MEADE was furious. Scarcely two months earlier, his victory at Gettysburg had made him the toast of the North. Now he was having almost as much trouble with pesky newsmen as he had had with Lee's Army of Northern Virginia. One day he forwarded some press clippings to his chief engineer, writing, "I should like to know who the correspondent is, & where he obtained his information." Meade was especially irate because the press reports told of violations of order and military propriety. All reporters were to be informed, Meade wrote, that further such reports "will result in their expulsion from this Army."

Meade's pique was understandable. The Civil War had proved a boon for journalism, especially in the North. A newspaper could sell five times its normal circulation after a big battle, and the Federal armies themselves could buy up as many as 25,000 copies of a single edition. The overwhelming public interest in the war, an interest fueled by circulation wars and the availability of news by telegraph, made the Civil War America's most important journalistic watershed.

Alas, the quality of the journalism was not equal to the challenge. One of the abler reporters, Sylvanus Cadwallader of the *New York Herald*, conceded in his memoirs that

> The first installment of correspondents sent to the armies deserved no high rank in public or official estimation. . . . Some were so lacking in conventional politeness as to make themselves positively disagreeable wherever they went. . . . And still others were sufficiently ignoble as to fasten themselves upon some colonel or brigadier, and [accept payment in return for] fulsome and undeserved praise of their patrons.

Some might regard Cadwallader's judgment as being on the generous side. Philip Knightly, in a study of war reporting over the years, concluded

33

that the vast majority of Northern correspondents were ignorant, dishonest, and unethical, and their dispatches often invented, partisan, and inflammatory. Good taste was rare, and objectivity not even a goal. One correspondent begged a dying Confederate for an interview, promising that if he had any last words "they will appear in my paper in the very best form." A reporter for the *New York World* told his wife that he had accepted $50 from an artillery officer in return for favorable mention in his column. "After all," he wrote home, "If ever a man needed $50 it is I."

Even allowing for the inflated rhetoric of the day, the quality of writing from the front was on a par with journalistic ethics. In the gingerbread prose of the 1860s, an inconclusive skirmish was an important victory; a battlefield rout became a strategic withdrawal; the army to which the correspondent was attached embodied all the heroic and manly virtues. A dead Confederate soldier was not merely a casualty, he was "sacrificed to the devilish ambitions of his implacable masters, Davis and Lee."

There were, perhaps, some mitigating circumstances. Field reporters endured the same privations of camp life as did the rank and file of both armies. In a war in which many generals became thoroughly confused, it is not surprising that battlefield reporting was less than accurate. And if reporting from the field was biased and partisan, so too were the papers for which the stories were written. The editor of the *La Crosse* (Wisconsin) *Democrat* thought nothing of proposing an epitaph for President Lincoln:

> Beneath this turf, the widow-maker lies,
> Little in everything, except in size.

The influence of the press was considerably greater in the 19th century than today, for there were no competing electronic media. Regionally, the press was more important in the North than in the South, for the greater urbanization of the North had made for larger as well as more numerous newspapers. In New York City alone there was a near-hysterical rivalry among Henry Raymond's *New York Times*, Horace Greeley's *Tribune*, and James Gordon Bennett's *Herald*. No Southern paper could approach the circulation of any of these three, and such papers as circulated in the Confederacy soon suffered from a shortage of newsprint and other materials as a result of the Federal blockade. And as the Federal armies advanced, more and more papers faced a choice between relocating or submitting to enemy authority. The immediate military danger to the Confederacy made most of its papers outspokenly patriotic and somewhat more amenable to direction than their powerful Yankee counterparts.

Reporters on both sides were obliged to consider what could or should be reported. Most were prepared to concede that information relating to troop movements should be kept out of the papers, but otherwise there were few guidelines. There was no strong sentiment that the people had a "right to know" all that went on; at the same time, none of America's previous conflicts provided a precedent for news censorship. And generals and politicians alike seemed to delight in making life difficult for reporters. Secretary of State Seward, for one, was fond of telling questioners, "If I didn't know, I would tell you."

Arrayed against the approximately 500 reporters who at one time or another covered the Union armies were a heterogeneous collection of generals, virtually none of whom had any experience in dealing with the press. At best they viewed reporters as a nuisance; more often, their lack of "conventional politeness" inspired stronger feelings. But among the generals there was a clear division between those who sought to exclude reporters from their lines and those who chose to conciliate the reporters and thereby "manage" the news.

Gen. George B. McClellan was one of the first to realize the importance of a good press. Not long after taking command of the Army of the Potomac in November 1861 he advised reporters that they should report as they pleased except about troop movements. McClellan may have gone even further. In conversation with a correspondent from the *New York Herald*, McClellan supposedly told how, at a recent cabinet meeting, he had been asked by President Lincoln to outline his plans for an offensive. This he had declined to do, McClellan told the reporter, but what he had declined to inform the president he would tell the influential *Herald*. After emphasizing his admiration for *Herald* publisher James Gordon Bennett, McClellan proceeded to outline his plans for the Peninsula campaign.

At the other end of the spectrum was the formidable and irascible William Tecumseh Sherman. Hypersensitive on the subject of spies, Sherman made little distinction between Northern journalists and enemy agents. In 1862 one newsman hoped to win the general's favor with a letter of introduction from Sherman's son, but his hopes were quickly dashed:

> "Letter from Tom, eh?" said Sherman. He read it, took out his watch and said: "It's eleven o'clock; the next train for Louisville goes at half-past one. Take that train! Be sure you take it; don't let me see you around here after it it's gone!"

> "But General! The people are anxious. I'm only after the truth."

> "We don't want the truth told about things here—that's what we *don't* want! Truth, eh? No, sir! We don't want to make the enemy any better informed than he is. Make no mistake about that train!"

One reporter, Thomas Knox of the *New York Herald*, became so fed up with Sherman and his censors that he submitted an uncleared account of the

Edwin Forbes's sketch, "Newspapers in Camp." *Author's Collection*

clash at Chickasaw Bluff in which he charged Sherman with bungling the attack and with denying hospital facilities to the wounded. After Sherman ordered that Knox be arrested and brought to headquarters, the reporter told Sherman, "Of course, General Sherman, I have no feeling against you personally, but you are regarded [as] the enemy of our set and we must in self-defense write you down."*

Correspondents in the West became bolder after the departure to Washington of Gen. Henry W. Halleck, who had largely excluded correspondents from his area of command. ("Whiskey flowed for correspondents," one of them wrote, "with the coming of Grant.")

The issue of censorship was clearly a sensitive one. The opposing armies read and spoke the same language. Newspapers passed freely across the lines. In the Atlantic Ocean, Confederate cruiser captains studied captured newspapers for the sailing schedules of Northern merchantmen. Robert E. Lee spent considerable time poring over the Northern press, and felt his time well spent. He was especially fond of the *Philadelphia Inquirer*, whose chief correspondent, Lee felt, knew what he reported and reported what he knew.

The telegraph added a new dimension to war reporting. At a time when one "scoop" could make a reporter famous, access to the telegraph could be the difference between success and failure. Early in the war, Secretary of War

---

*The clash between Sherman and Knox is treated in greater detail in the next chapter.

Edwin M. Stanton appointed the president of the American Telegraph Company, Edward Sanford, supervisor of telegrams. Although there was some grumbling, most people believed that military control of the telegraph was, under the circumstances, necessary and appropriate.

Unfortunately, control of telegraph traffic did not end security leaks. Therefore, in February 1862 Stanton ordered that any paper publishing military information "not expressly authorized" would be denied the privilege of receiving news reports by telegraph or shipping its papers by rail. The ensuing protest was so vigorous that Stanton modified his order so as to permit publication of "past facts" that did not reveal the strength or location of Federal units.

Fortunately for Stanton, the correspondents accompanying an army in the field were subject to military law and liable to trial by court-martial for any offenses. Particularly useful was that section of the Articles of War that forbade "holding correspondence with, or giving intelligence to, the enemy, either directly or indirectly." But the articles were in no sense uniformly applied; bureaucrats and generals were often more interested in disseminating information that placed them in a favorable light than in protecting secrets. When Federal forces gained a victory, no one was more eager than Lincoln to see that word got around. One evening, while talking to a reporter, Lincoln received two telegrams from the West, both containing good news. Lincoln, pen in hand, said that his visitors could have copies of both. "I'll copy the short one while you copy the long one, as you write much faster than I."

So much for handling the good news. When news was bad, Secretary Stanton was prone to tamper with casualty figures. The War Department withheld news of the fall of Harper's Ferry during the Gettysburg campaign, and then reported the number of Federal troops captured at 4,000, rather than the 11,200 that had actually been taken. By May 1864 the War Department had taken to issuing regular news handouts. But the casualties incurred by Grant's army were so disheartening that Stanton on one occasion reduced Federal casualties to about one-third the actual number. Stanton has been described as the father of the official communique; considering his record, it was an inauspicious beginning.

More often than not, control of the press was lax. Although sometimes denied access to the telegraph, reporters wrote their dispatches without hindrance. Couriers came and went at will, and papers were largely uninhibited in what they wrote of a long succession of Federal setbacks on the battlefield. A few reporters were dealt with under the Articles of War, but they were very much the exception. At a time when the country's life was at stake, the press was free almost to the point of license.

When the brass did not care for what was being reported, their best leverage was after the fact. Although columns were at first unsigned and later often signed with initials or pseudonyms, those at the front knew who was reporting what. Reporters who fell into disfavor could be dealt with in a number of ways, including the denial of the fringe benefits attendant to the officers' mess.

The Confederacy suffered far less from leaks than the Union did, but it was not entirely immune. Early in the war the *New York Herald*, working from Southern newspapers, published figures on Confederate strength that Jefferson Davis's secretary of war characterized as being as accurate as his own. As time went on, however, Southern security improved. Reporting of troop movements was strictly prohibited, and the Confederate commanders were more successful than their Federal counterparts in keeping reporters out of their lines. The law provided stiff penalties against editors who published secret information or reports calculated to impair confidence in the Confederacy's military leaders.

On occasion, the Confederates used the press as a vehicle for misinformation. During the Peninsula campaign, Lee became aware that McClellan, like Lee himself, made a practice of studying the "enemy" press. Therefore, after ordering Gen. "Stonewall" Jackson to march from the Shenandoah Valley to help defend Richmond, Lee asked the Richmond papers to report that reinforcements were being sent to Jackson in the Valley.

Although battlefield casualties among reporters were uncommon, the turnover in correspondents was enormous. Charles Coffin of the *Boston Journal* is said to have been the only reporter who covered the war from beginning to end. But as the war went on, the quality of the reporting improved. The fortunes of war occasionally placed an able reporter in a position to describe an important event, and Whitelaw Reid's description of the Battle of Shiloh and George Smalley's description of the clash at Antietam were stories that transcended the Victorian prose of the day.

One of the war's more poignant stories relates to Lincoln's concern for Grant's army after it disappeared into the Virginia "wilderness" in May 1864. The telegraph was silent, and Washington abounded with rumors that Lee had sprung a trap on his antagonist. Then came word that a cub reporter for the *New York Tribune*, 19-year-old Henry Wing, had been detained by Federal troops at Union Mills, about 20 miles from Washington. In return for permission to telegraph 100 words to the *Tribune*, Wing agreed to tell Lincoln and his cabinet what he had seen.

Wing's report was inconclusive, for he had seen only a small portion of the fighting and his information was some 36 hours old. After hearing him out, the members of Lincoln's cabinet returned to their own offices; only Wing remained.

"You wanted to speak to me?" Lincoln asked.

"Yes, Mr. President. I have a message for you—a message from

General Grant. He told me I was to give it to you when you were alone."

"Something from Grant to me?"

"Yes," Wing replied without hesitation. "He told me I was to tell you, Mr. President, that there would be no turning back." Grant had led him aside just as he was about to leave headquarters on Friday morning and had charged him with this message.

This was such a message as Lincoln had been waiting for through three long years of war. Impulsively he passed his long arm around Wing's shoulders and kissed his cheek.

The Federals' improving military prospects did not bring a comparable improvement in relations between the military and the press. William Swinton of the *New York Times* was expelled from the Army of the Potomac in 1864 after a variety of offenses, including being caught eavesdropping on a conversation between Grant and Meade. Not surprisingly, one of the bitterest incidents was precipitated by the acerbic Meade. Meade was infuriated by a dispatch from the *Philadelphia Inquirer* correspondent, Edward Crapsey, which alleged incorrectly that Meade had counseled retreat after a recent brush between the Army of the Potomac and Lee's army. Not content with expelling Crapsey, Meade—whose loathing for the press was second only to Sherman's—ordered him drummed out of the lines to the "Rogue's March," facing backwards on a mule.

The "Bohemian Brigade" of reporters, which was not noted for its unity, in this instance rallied around Crapsey. It was agreed in a correspondents' meeting that henceforth Meade's name would be mentioned in dispatches only in connection with a defeat. The Army of the Potomac became "Grant's army," a term by which it is widely remembered today, despite the fact that Grant left its day-to-day operations to Meade. This silent treatment continued for six months, after which time reporter Sylvanus Cadwallader, among others, took the lead in restoring Meade to grace. Meade himself conceded, in retrospect, that his punishment of Crapsey had been excessive.

There were no polls in 1865 to indicate what the public thought of its newspapers or its reporters. One suspects that, having no standard of comparison, most readers were impressed by the speed of telegraphic reporting, and tolerated biased dispatches so long as they coincided with the reader's own prejudices. The publishers, for their part, were euphoric about the prosperity that the war had brought to newspaper row. James Gordon Bennett rhapsodized, "The United States, the City of New York and the *New York Herald* have a future compared to which the present is nothing."

George G. Meade in an uncharacteristically benign pose. *Library of Congress*

William Tecumseh Sherman would have offered a different perspective. The story goes that when, during the war, Sherman was told that three correspondents had been lost in battle, he remarked, "Good! Now we shall have news from hell before breakfast!"

CHAPTER 7

———

The Bizarre Court-Martial of
Thomas Knox

WILLIAM TECUMSEH SHERMAN did not care for reporters. That quick-tempered soldier viewed them, at best, as able-bodied citizens who should be in uniform but chose instead to view the war from a position of relative safety while enjoying such amenities as the war had to offer. At worst, the eloquent Sherman characterized them as "buzzards" and "paid spies."

Apart from an instinctive dislike for civilians who were paid to second-guess his decisions, Sherman had solid grounds for his dislike of the press. For one thing, he was convinced that reports in the Northern press were an important source of intelligence for the enemy. On one occasion he wrote his wife, "We look in vain to [Confederate] newspapers for scraps from which to guess at the disposition of their forces . . . [while] everything we do or attempt to do is paraded in all our newspapers."

Some very distasteful personal encounters with the press also influenced Sherman's thinking. In October 1861, a newsman who had eavesdropped on a conference between Sherman and Secretary of War Simon Cameron had subsequently spread stories that Cameron regarded Sherman as "unbalanced." Two months later, while Sherman was on leave, the *Cincinnati Commercial* ran a sensational article stating flatly that Sherman was insane and had been removed from his command. The mercurial Sherman indeed appears to have been the target of a deliberate campaign by some reporters to bring about his ouster; if the general was a bit paranoid on the subject of the press, he had his reasons.

But these problems had arisen early in the war, and since then his fortunes had taken a turn for the better. He had distinguished himself at the Battle of Shiloh, and in May 1862 had been promoted to major general of volunteers. Shortly after Grant took charge of the Army of the Tennessee, Sherman found himself in command of 40,000 men with whom to move against the Confederate fortress at Vicksburg.

41

Gen. William T.
Sherman in
about 1863.
Library of Congress

Sherman, with his headquarters in Memphis, was ready to march in early December. Before doing so, he issued General Order No. 8, which was in the best Sherman tradition. In it he ordered that all civilians except those on the army payroll be excluded from the areas under his command. Lest there be any misunderstanding on the part of reporters, he specified that anyone writing for publication from his lines would be arrested for conveying information to the enemy and be treated as a spy.

This was strong medicine, but it did not deter the more enterprising reporters. More than 20 correspondents managed to attach themselves to Sherman's expedition, several of them displaying passes from General Grant. Once his campaign was under way, Sherman had more immediate problems than dealing with the press. On December 29 he attacked the Confederate-held bluffs north of Vicksburg near Chickasaw Bayou. The Rebels were strongly entrenched, and Sherman withdrew after suffering some 1,800 casualties in a series of badly coordinated attacks.

One of the reporters who filed a report on the battle was Thomas Knox of the *New York Herald*. According to Knox, the attack had been a complete fiasco; Sherman had specified no time for the assault, and there was widespread confusion among his division and brigade commanders. Moreover, the commanding general had shown himself callous to the suffering of his wounded. In a section that infuriated Sherman, Knox wrote,

> By some criminal oversight, there had been little preparation for battle on the part of Sherman's medical director, and the hospitals were but poorly supplied with many needed stores. Since the battle, General Sherman has persistently refused to allow a hospital boat to go above, although [detention of the wounded] in this region is daily fatal to many lives. The only known reason for his refusal is his fear that a knowledge of his mismanagement will reach the papers of the North.

Knox's dispatch was not published until January 18, 1863, in part because of problems in getting his copy into the mails and out of the reach of Sherman's staff. Other "illegal" correspondents also filed stories on Chickasaw, none of them flattering to the army commander but none quite in the same class as Knox's hatchet job. In any case Sherman saw an opportunity: If an example could be made of Knox, who represented one of the largest papers in the country, might not his fate serve as an example to other reporters? On January 31, Sherman ordered Knox brought before him.

Thomas Knox was a burly 27-year-old who had taught school in New Hampshire before attracting the attention of publisher James Gordon Bennett with some stories on the Civil War in Missouri. Some found Knox to be aggressive and overbearing, but there is little to suggest that he differed greatly in this respect from other reporters. Abrasive or not, Knox was not easily bullied. Face to face with the choleric Sherman, Knox defended his Chickasaw dispatch, telling Sherman in the language reported in the preceding chapter, "Of course, General Sherman, I had no feeling against you personally, but you are regarded [as] the enemy of our set, and we must in self-defense write you down."

This remark may have sealed Knox's fate. Sherman wrote to Admiral Porter,

> I am going to have the correspondent of the *New York Herald* tried by court-martial as a spy, not that I want the fellow shot, but because I want to establish the principle that such people cannot attend our armies, in violation of orders, and defy us, publishing their garbled statements and defaming officers who are doing their best.

Knox knew that he was in trouble, and he may have suspected that Sherman was quite capable of having him shot. On February 1 he wrote a letter to Sherman that in effect retracted his Chickasaw dispatch. "I find to my regret," Knox wrote, "that I labored under repeated errors, and made in consequence several misstatements, which I now take pleasure in correcting." On reflection, Knox concluded that no blame attached to Sherman in connection with the setback at Chickasaw Bayou.

The retraction was to no avail. On February 6, Knox was brought before a court-martial aboard the gunboat *Warsaw* at Young's Point, Louisiana. The Army claimed jurisdiction over Knox on the same grounds that it regulated sutlers and prostitutes; the formal charges described him as "a citizen and camp-follower." But the Knox trial was clearly out of the ordinary. It would prove to be the only court-martial of a reporter in the Civil War, and it attracted wide interest.

There were three charges: that Knox's Chickasaw dispatch constituted giving information to the enemy, that Knox was a spy as defined by Sherman's General Order No. 8, and that Knox's having joined the expedition to Chickasaw constituted disobedience to orders.

Although the first two charges may have seemed excessive, the army was not without a case. Knox's dispatch had cited a number of Federal units by name, providing information that might have been useful to the enemy. But was Knox in fact a spy, even if he met the technical definition of one? The prosecution pointed out that Knox had been warned by Sherman's general order, which included a sentence, "Any person whatever, whether in the service of the United States or transports, found making reports for publication which might reach the enemy giving them aid and comfort, will be arrested and treated as spies." Clearly, Knox had defied Sherman's order.

As for the third charge, the army contended that Knox had knowingly disobeyed not only Sherman's order but an earlier War Department directive specifying that all dispatches relating to military movements must be cleared by the district commander.

President of the seven-member court was Brig. Gen. John M. Thayer, later a U.S. senator from Nebraska. The principals were all drawn from Sherman's command, but this did not prevent Knox's counsel, Lt. Col. William B. Woods, from mounting a spirited defense. With regard to the first charge, Woods pointed out that in the East correspondents had been permitted to mention units by name *after* an action had taken place, much as Knox had done.

After two weeks of testimony and deliberation, the court acquitted Knox of the first two charges but found him guilty of disobedience to orders. He was sentenced to be expelled from the line of the Army of the Tennessee, and he was to stay away on penalty of imprisonment. Sherman was far from mollified; he thought the sentence far too light and dismissal of the spying charge unwarranted. Must the army prove that a press dispatch had actually reached the enemy to prove that a correspondent was aiding the enemy?

Knox and his allies, of course, viewed the sentence in quite a different light. Members of the Washington press corps gained an audience with

President Lincoln, to whom they stressed their confidence in Knox's loyalty. The president observed, in reply, that he was prepared to suspend Knox's banishment if Grant would concur. In a memorandum of March 20, 1863, Lincoln wrote that Knox's sentence was to be suspended long enough for Knox to travel to Grant's headquarters and make his case.

Grant himself was not above cultivating the press, but he did not hesitate when Knox showed up with Lincoln's memo. His choice was between the transient gratitude of the *New York Herald* and, perhaps, the services of his ablest subordinate. The letter that Grant wrote to Knox cemented a lifelong friendship with the volatile Sherman:

> The letter of the President of the United States authorizing you to return to these headquarters, and to remain with my consent . . . has been shown me.
>
> You came here first in positive violation of an order from General Sherman. Because you were not pleased with his treatment of army followers, who had violated his order, you attempted to break down his influence with his command, and to blast his reputation with the public. You made insinuations against his sanity, and said many things which were untrue, and, so far as your [dispatch] had influence, calculated to affect the public service unfavorably.
>
> General Sherman is one of the ablest soldiers and purest men in the country. You have attacked him and been sentenced to expulsion from this department for the offense. Whilst I would conform to the slightest wish of the President, where it is formed upon a fair representation of both sides of any question, my respect for General Sherman is such that in this case I must decline, unless General Sherman first gives his consent to your remaining.

This letter should have brought the Knox affair to a conclusion. Somewhat naively, however, Knox saw the final clause of Grant's letter as a door slightly ajar. He forwarded a copy of Lincoln's memorandum to Sherman, with a note that characterized Grant as agreeable to his return. But the newsman could have spared himself the trouble. Sherman replied,

> Come with a sword or musket in your hand, prepared to share with us our fate in sunshine and storm, in prosperity and adversity, in plenty and scarcity, and I will welcome you as a brother and associate; but come as you now do . . . as the representative of the press, which as you yourself say makes so slight a distinction between truth and falsehood, and my answer is, Never.

Knox continued for a time on the *Herald*'s payroll, but the war largely passed him by. He reached Gettysburg too late to report on the battle itself, and he was not assigned to any other important campaign. Although the *Herald* may have feared discrimination by the army against Knox, the fact is that the war saw an enormous turnover among reporters, as the first group of newsmen gave way to more qualified successors. In any case, Knox continued his writing career. His postwar publications included a history of the Republican Party, a campaign biography of presidential candidate James G. Blaine, and a series of travel books, including one that led to his being awarded the Order of the White Elephant by the King of Siam.

In a book of war stories published in 1865, Knox offered a slightly bowdlerized account of his clash with Sherman. There is no mention of his verbal provocation of the general, or of the acknowledged inaccuracies in his initial dispatch about Chickasaw. Nor did he touch upon his cringing apology to Sherman when trial appeared imminent. Rather, Knox suggests that the incident was a regrettable misunderstanding, one recalled in sorrow but not in anger.

Sherman, in his own memoirs, makes no explicit mention of the Knox case. But as he wrote in 1875, he was no less concerned about the proper role for the press than he had been in wartime. Interestingly, the final paragraph of this two-volume work deals with this issue, in perhaps the most restrained language of which Sherman was capable:

> Newspaper correspondents with an army, as a rule, are mischievous. They are the world's gossips, pick up and retail the camp scandal, and generally drift to the headquarters of some general who finds it easier to make a reputation at home than with his own corps or division. . . . Yet so greedy are the people at large for war news, that it is doubtful whether any army commander can exclude all reporters, without bringing down on himself a clamor that may imperil his own safety. Time and moderation must bring a just solution to this modern difficulty.

CHAPTER 8

▬

Farewell to the *Monitor*

ACCORDING TO the schoolbooks, John Ericsson's famous ironclad was called the "cheesebox on a raft." Others, however, used less buoyant metaphors, including that of a flatiron. While the *Monitor* was being rushed to completion in Brooklyn, she was examined by a Navy Department designer, John Lenthall. Although impressed with the vessel's fighting potential, Lenthall asked Ericsson how such a low-lying iron ship could support a huge turret, munitions, and some 60 sailors. When Ericsson insisted that heavy seas would merely pass over her, Lenthall was unconvinced. The ship was an "iron pot," he pronounced, and her inventor crazy.[1]

John Ericsson may not have been crazy, but his design for a floating turret sacrificed seagoing qualities for armor and striking power. Basically, Ericsson's creation had two hulls. The lower hull was designed to be underwater; the upper hull, some five feet high, overlapped it, and was heavily armored. In the center of the deck was the ship's offensive punch, a revolving turret 9 feet high and 20 feet across, mounting two 11-inch guns. The turret was moved by a donkey engine and a system of gears in the lower hull.

The speed with which the *Monitor* was built grew out of reports that the Confederates were working on an ironclad of their own, as indeed they were. The most important challenge facing the Confederate Navy Department was that of keeping the South's ports open, and Secretary of the Navy Stephen Mallory was fully aware of what might be accomplished by a few ironclads. The Confederates were said to be converting a U.S. Navy ship of the line, the *Merrimack*, into an ironclad, and work on Ericsson's counterpart proceeded in an atmosphere of near frenzy.

The *Monitor* was launched in her Brooklyn shipyard on January 30, 1862, amid cheers from a crowd which, however, included a few skeptics. All went well. A boatman who went out on the river in the belief that he might be needed to rescue survivors returned empty-handed. A reporter wrote some-

47

what defensively, "It was evident even to the dullest observer that the battery hadn't the slightest intention of sinking."[2]

On March 6, Secretary of the Navy Gideon Welles ordered the *Monitor*'s newly designated commander, Lt. John L. Worden, to bring his vessel to Washington, anchoring below Alexandria. The ironclad left Brooklyn that same day, towed by a steam tug. Seas were moderate on the trip down the coast, but the *Monitor* demonstrated some unsettling tendencies. Although small waves did in fact flow across her deck, larger ones battered the turret and pilot house, springing leaks and causing minor damage. One of her officers reported to Secretary Welles, "She has not the steam power to go against a head wind or sea."[3] Nevertheless, the *Monitor* was towed successfully, first to Washington and then to Newport News.

Nothing that the *Monitor* did before or after her famous encounter with the *Merrimack* could detract from that epic confrontation on March 9, 1862. The day before, the newly armored *Merrimack*, renamed *Virginia* by the Confederates, had wreaked havoc among the wooden hulls of the Federal fleet. In the space of a few hours the Confederate ironclad had destroyed the sloop *Cumberland* and the screw frigate *Congress*. She appeared certain to continue her rampage the following day, only to be confronted by Ericsson's "flatiron."

The duel between ironclads that ensued was inconclusive. The two ships battered one another for four hours without inflicting serious damage. But it was the North that felt relief at the drawn battle, for the *Monitor* alone had stood in the way of naval disaster. The fact that the clash off Hampton Roads had made all wooden warships obsolescent seemed less important at the time.

Although there were no fatalities aboard the *Monitor*, one injury would contribute to the eventual fate of the Federal ironclad. Skipper John Worden had been sighting through one of the viewing slits when a heavy shot struck the pilot house, throwing particles into his eyes and causing temporary blindness. After the battle Worden was sent to Washington, where his wounds were treated and he was lionized by the Lincoln administration. In time he would be given command of a new ironclad, but this was of no help to the *Monitor*. When orders came that would place that vessel in imminent peril, the one voice that might have been heeded with respect to her lack of seaworthiness was not to be heard.

The *Monitor* spent the remainder of 1862 in Hampton Roads. Her most important responsibility ended in May when McClellan's advance on Norfolk obliged the Confederates to destroy the *Merrimack*. The first of the antagonists in the historic battle of March 9, 1862, was no more.

The *Monitor* undertook some incidental missions in the bay area, but her deep draft and poor maneuverability made her a doubtful asset. Most of the time, navy authorities worried about a Rebel attempt to seize or sabotage

The *Monitor's* turret, showing damage from the engagement with the *Merrimack*.
Naval History Division

her, while the *Monitor's* crew grumbled at living conditions aboard an iron
vessel in which temperatures below decks sometimes reached 160 degrees
Fahrenheit. In October she was towed to the Washington Navy Yard for a
refit; while there, the *Monitor* was the object of considerable scrutiny. President Lincoln inspected her, as did Secretary Welles. So did the public. "They
went through the ship," wrote Acting Master Louis Stodder, "like a flock of
magpies, prying loose as souvenirs anything removable. When we came to
clean up at night there was not a key, doorknob, escutcheon—there wasn't a
thing that hadn't been carried away."[4]

In due course the ironclad returned to Hampton Roads with a new skipper, 41-year-old John P. Bankhead. Bankhead was a respected officer in the
Old Navy, but he had none of Worden's interest in ironclads. The change in
commanders was replicated elsewhere; not only was her skipper new, only
20 crewmen of her original complement remained.

The *Monitor* returned to Hampton Roads amid rumors that the Rebels
were about to launch a major effort aimed at breaking the Federal blockade

of Wilmington, North Carolina. Welles should probably have known better than to commit his only proven ironclad to the perils of Cape Hatteras. But war entails risks, and the need for the *Monitor*'s services off Wilmington appeared compelling. On Christmas Eve, Welles issued orders for the supply ship *Rhode Island*, a converted yacht, to tow the ironclad to Wilmington. Bad weather delayed the sailing, but by December 29 the skies had cleared. The day was chill but clear, and there was a crowd at the Newport News waterfront: Federal soldiers in their coats, dock workers, and even a few curious Virginians. Whatever one might think of the Yankees, it was not every day that one viewed the departure of a vessel like the *Monitor*.

By 6:00 P.M. the *Rhode Island* and the *Monitor* had passed Cape Henry, making about five knots. Darkness fell, but the good weather held; only in the morning was there increased swell, and a slight increase in wind force. Rain came, but the crew of the *Monitor* felt no special concern. Their ship was riding well, and in any case it was equipped with no fewer than three sets of pumps, devices that together were capable of handling up to 2,000 gallons per minute. Early in the afternoon of the December 30, the *Monitor* and her escort passed 14 miles east of the Cape Hatteras light. The ship's paymaster, William Keeler, later recalled, "At 5 o'clock P.M. we sat down to dinner, each one cheerful & happy & though the sea was rolling & foaming . . . the laugh & jest passed freely 'round."[5]

By evening, however, there was cause for concern. The sky was dirty, the wind was fresh, the sea stronger. The *Monitor* began shipping water in some volume, obliging Captain Bankhead to activate two of his sets of pumps. His vessel began to plunge and yaw; to those aboard the *Rhode Island*, the *Monitor* seemed at times to disappear altogether. In the hope that his ship would ride better out of tow, Bankhead ordered the tow rope severed. This proved to be an error, for the underpowered ironclad proved unable to keep her bow to the storm. Few sailors—and Bankhead was not among them—had much experience in handling an ironclad under storm conditions.

It was clear that floating was not the *Monitor*'s strong suit. When she was carried up by a wave, the undersurface of the upper hull would come down with great force, loosening plates and pressing water into the hull. Heavy seas rolled over the pilot house and crashed into the always leaky turret. More water entered by way of the sighting slits in the pilot house and blower pipes to the engines. By 10:00 P.M. the third and last set of pumps had been activated.

At 10:30 P.M., with seven inches of water in the engine room, Bankhead hoisted a distress signal and asked the *Rhode Island* to send boats. It was a difficult rescue, made more so by the fact that the *Monitor* had stowed her own boats aboard the *Rhode Island*. Such steam as the *Monitor* could muster was required for the pumps; the ship herself was not under control and several times threatened to swamp boats from the *Rhode Island*. The ironclad was almost invisible from her consort, recognizable only by the distress lantern atop the turret.

Quartermaster Richard Najier was still at his post at the *Monitor*'s helm. Bankhead shouted for him to abandon ship. "No, sir," Najier shouted back, "Not until you go!"[6]

Paymaster Keeler started to rescue the ship's accounts, but realized that he would never make it back with an armload of ledgers. He climbed to the deck hoping to find a boat:

> It was a scene well calculated to appall the boldest heart. Mountains of water were rushing across our decks & foaming along our sides; the small boats were pitching & tossing about on them or crashing against our sides, mere playthings on the billows. The howling of the tempest, the roar & dash of the waters; the hoarse orders through the speaking trumpets of the officers . . . & the whole scene lit up by the ghastly glare of the blue lights burning on our consort, formed a panorama of horror which time can never efface from my memory.[7]

Finding his vessel filling rapidly, Bankhead ordered all those still on board, about 25 or 30 men, to get into two boats from the *Rhode Island*. The two boats approached very cautiously, for the sea was breaking over the *Monitor*'s submerged deck with great force, washing several men overboard. Many sailors on the ironclad refused to leave the false security of her turret. "Feeling that I had done everything in my power to save the vessel and crew," Bankhead wrote, "I jumped into the already deeply laden boat and left the *Monitor*, whose heavy, sluggish motion gave evidence that she could float but a short time longer."[8]

By some standards, Bankhead's behavior might appear less than heroic. He left his vessel while 16 men remained on board—men who would go down with the ship. The survivors, however, were not inclined to be critical. Among the *Monitor*'s green crew were several sailors who refused to leave the ironclad for the *Rhode Island*'s storm-tossed boats. Others were unable or unwilling to come up from inside the ship. The consensus appeared to be that Bankhead had stayed with his ship for as long as he could find crewmen who would enter a boat.

From the *Rhode Island*, exhausted survivors stared across the black water. From time to time the lantern on the *Monitor*'s turret would swing into view, only to disappear once more. At 1:30 A.M. it flickered one last time, then slid under the waves.

The loss of the *Monitor* was one more blow to the North, for whom the land war was going badly enough. Secretary Welles, who bore a good share of the blame for the ironclad's ill-starred voyage, felt her loss keenly. Yet there were no recriminations, and the navy was charitable toward the *Monitor*'s last commander. Bankhead remained on the active list, and in 1864 was commanding the gunboat *Oswego* in the Roanoke River when she was sunk by a Confederate mine. At war's end he was commanding the screw sloop *Wyoming*, one of a number of U.S. Navy ships that searched, unsuccessfully, for the Confederate cruiser *Shenandoah*.

So it was that by the end of 1862 both of the ironclads that had done so much to revolutionize naval warfare had gone to the bottom. The *Merrimack* was past reclaiming, but what of her adversary? The *Rhode Island* had taken a fix on her final position, and the *Monitor* was never entirely forgotten. Over the years, in the shallow waters off Diamond Shoals, there were several false sightings of the wreck, and there were always historians and marine archaeologists who wished to see John Ericsson's creation located, raised, and properly enshrined.

In the summer of 1973 the Duke University Marine Laboratory embarked on a systematic search for the *Monitor*. Employing the research ship *Eastward*, and assisted by the National Geographic Society, a research team led by John G. Newton scrutinized an area of seabed five by eight miles, employing sonar, underwater cameras, and magnetometers. After two weeks of searching they located the ironclad in 220 feet of water, some 15 miles off Diamond Shoals light. Final verification came when a mosaic of underwater photographs showed what was unmistakably the encrusted *Monitor*, resting upside down on her massive turret.

The wreck was found to be in such fragile condition that it could not be raised. But, fittingly, the *Monitor*'s final resting place was subsequently dedicated as a marine sanctuary.

CHAPTER 9

"With More Sorrow Than I Can Tell"

Eᴀʀʟʏ ON the afternoon of January 24, 1863, a lone horseman slogged his way through a clutch of army tents to the headquarters of Maj. Gen. William S. Rosecrans on a hill outside Murfreesboro, Tennessee. The hill was not a beehive of activity. Other than an occasional dispatch rider, there was little to suggest that Murfreesboro was occupied by a 50,000 man Federal force, Rosecrans's Army of the Cumberland.

The lone horseman was no ordinary rider, but an important addition to Rosecrans's staff. Brig. Gen. James A. Garfield was not a soldier by profession; born on an Ohio farm, he had obtained a college education and then become a preacher and a college professor. When war came, the thirty-year-old Garfield was a member of the Ohio senate, from which he resigned to recruit a regiment. The amateur soldier proved a fast learner, and he was lucky. In January 1862 Gen. Don Carlos Buell put him in command of a brigade with orders to check a Confederate force that was attempting to enter eastern Kentucky from Virginia. The resulting clash at Middle Creek proved inconclusive, but it was the Confederates who retreated, and Garfield became a local celebrity. In November 1862 he was elected to the U.S. Congress but because he was unable, under the laws of the day, to take his seat until December 1863, he became available for assignment to Rosecrans.

The commander to whom he reported would prove to be one of the paradoxes of the Union armies. William Starke Rosecrans, forty-four, combined personal bravery and strategic acumen to a degree rarely found in either army. Like Garfield, he was an Ohioan, and, like Garfield, he had had some early successes that had marked him for speedy advancement. Unlike Garfield, he was a West Pointer and a professional soldier. Rosecrans won new laurels in the fall of 1862, when his corps repulsed a Confederate attempt to recapture Corinth, Mississippi. After succeeding Buell as com-

Eng.ᵈbyA.H.Ritchie

Future president James A. Garfield as a major general of volunteers. *Author's Collection*

mander of the Army of the Cumberland in October 1862, Rosecrans had delighted the administration in Washington with an advance into eastern Tennessee. On December 31 he had incurred more than 13,000 casualties in holding off Bragg at Stone's River, it was the Rebels, not the Yankees, who eventually left the field.

In January 1863, Rosecrans's army was still recuperating from the recent carnage at Stone's River. On the Federal side, only the skill of Rosecrans, George H. Thomas, and Phil Sheridan had prevented Bragg's advance from turning into a rout. Stone's River would prove to be the most deadly battle of the war in terms of the numbers engaged, and members of Rosecrans's staff still spoke in hushed tones of Col. Julius Garesche, the army's popular chief of staff, who had been decapitated by a Rebel shell. Now there were reports to be written, supplies to be ordered.

Unlike Garfield, Rosecrans was a military professional opposed to anything that smacked of politics in the army. "Old Rosey" was a hard fighter, a devout Catholic, and a convivial friend. A prominent newsman of the day,

Whitelaw Reid, characterized him as notably accessible and totally lacking in pretense: "In the field he was capable of immense labor; he seemed never to grow weary and never to need sleep. Few officers have been more popular with their commands, or have inspired more confidence in the rank and file." But there was another side to this catalog of virtues. For Rosecrans—unable to pace himself, and perhaps lacking confidence in his staff—operated in a constant state of nervous fatigue that would eventually lead to disaster.

When Garfield reported to the Army of the Cumberland at Murfreesboro, he and Rosecrans hit it off immediately. "He is the most Spanish looking man I know," Garfield wrote his wife, "and although he swears fiercely, he is a Jesuit of the highest style of roman piety. He carries a rosary attached

Gen. William S. Rosecrans, who thought that James A. Garfield had descended "from honor to infamy." *National Archives*

to his watch dial." As the army recuperated from Stone's River, there was time for relaxed conversation, and Garfield came to enjoy theological discussions with a Catholic protagonist. The association with Rosecrans led Garfield to question some of his earlier prejudices about West Pointers. He wrote to his sponsor in Washington, Secretary of the Treasury Salmon P. Chase, "I . . . am glad to tell you that I believe in him, that he is sound to the bone on the great questions of the war, and the way it should be conducted. . . . If the country and the government will stand by him I feel sure he will justify their highest expectations."[1]

With the arrival of Garfield, Rosecrans had acquired an intelligent subordinate who reflected the zeal found in the best of volunteer officers of the war. He was sober, hard-working, and literate—all qualities Rosecrans was in a position to appreciate. Garfield was, in addition, an ambitious congressman-elect with friends in Washington and definite ideas as to how the war should be fought. But if some members of Rosecrans's staff viewed Garfield as a spy from the War Department, the young officer soon won them over. He worked hard, had a ready laugh, and enjoyed the companionship of an army in the field.

Garfield had hoped to be given command of a division, but he was offered instead the post of army chief of staff, which had been vacant since Stone's River. Garfield was in no hurry to accept. He knew that Rosecrans's relations with the War Department were strained, and that too close an association with "Old Rosey" could be a political liability. But once he accepted the position offered him he went to work with gusto.

In June 1863 the Army of the Cumberland consisted of some 50,000 men—40,000 infantry, 6,800 cavalry, and 3,100 artillery—divided into corps commanded by generals Alexander McCook, Thomas L. Crittenden, and George H. Thomas. As chief of staff, Garfield was responsible for the drafting and delivery of his commanding officer's orders to units of an often scattered command. His job involved little strategy or glamour but a great deal of paperwork.

Southeast of the Army of the Cumberland, at Tullahoma, Tennessee, lay the Confederate army of the acerbic Braxton Bragg. Bragg's army was perhaps 13,000 men smaller than the Army of the Cumberland, but his cavalry was markedly superior to anything available to the Yankees. Rosecrans himself was aggressive, but he had seen enough of what Bedford Forrest and Joe Wheeler could do to his communications to be wary. Not until six months after Stone's River did Rosecrans put his army in motion, and even then he did so less from conviction than from realization that he could expect no cavalry reinforcements. This cautious course had Garfield's approval. In a letter to Chase written in April, Garfield wrote that "it is useless to advance into rebel territory, unless we are prepared to hold the ground we win in battle."

Garfield continued to respect his commander's reasons for caution, but his patience was wearing thin. In Washington, too, there was concern not only at Rosecrans's procrastination, but over the possibility that continued inaction by the Army of the Cumberland might enable the Confederates to concentrate against Grant at Vicksburg. In early June Rosecrans professed to be ready, but when Secretary of War Edwin Stanton withdrew a corps from his command, Rosecrans insisted on a reassessment. On June 8 he sent a memorandum to his corps and division commanders, asking their views as to the wisdom of an advance. All 17 polled, including the redoubtable George H. Thomas, opposed an immediate advance, in part because they could find no evidence that Bragg was sending reinforcements to Vicksburg.

In relying so heavily on the consensus of his commanders, Rosecrans may have lost some of his luster in the eyes of his chief of staff. Garfield had not been included in the poll, which was limited to troop commanders, but his views were well known to Rosecrans. The younger man was so vexed at the army's failure to move that he sent Rosecrans a long memorandum in which he listed no fewer than nine arguments for an immediate advance. "I refuse to entertain a doubt," he wrote, "that this army, which in January last defeated Bragg's superior numbers, cannot overwhelm his present greatly inferior force." Part of the problem was that no one was quite sure how many troops Bragg had. In fact, Bragg had about 50,000 effectives, about 10,000 fewer than Rosecrans. Thus the Rebel force was inferior to that of the Federals, but not "greatly inferior."

By late June Rosecrans was ready, and his campaign against Tullahoma, once begun, showed a sure hand. Avoiding a frontal move against Bragg's hilltop entrenchments, the Federal commander swung his army to the east, outflanking the Confederates. Each of Rosecrans's four infantry corps marched through a different gap in the Cumberland foothills, forcing Bragg to concentrate initially at Tullahoma. Rosecrans's march was made in some of the heaviest rain of the war, and Crittenden's corps required four days to cover one 21-mile stretch. The slowness of the Federal advance permitted Bragg to retire in good order, and Garfield, for one, felt that the rains had prevented the Army of the Cumberland from striking a decisive blow. Nevertheless, on June 30 Bragg began a withdrawal from Tullahoma toward Chattanooga. On the same July 4 that saw the fall of Vicksburg, Rosecrans was able to report an end to organized Confederate resistance in eastern Tennessee.

From Tullahoma, Rosecrans carried on petulant dialogue with the War Department over what to do next. He argued for a joint offensive with Grant against Bragg's army, but Halleck vetoed this promising course. Meanwhile, Garfield chaffed at the army's inaction, unburdening himself with a letter to Secretary Chase on July 27:

I have for a long time wanted to write you, not only to acknowledge your last kind letter, but to say some things confidentially on
the movements in this department. . . .

I cannot conceal from you the fact that I have been greatly tried
and dissatisfied with the slow progress we have made in this department since the battle of Stones River. [Not] that the one hun-
dred and sixty-two days which elapsed between the battle of
Stones River and the next advance of this army were spent in
idleness or trifling . . . but for many weeks prior to our late movement, I could not but feel that there was not that live and earnest
determination to fling the great weight of this army into the scale
and make its power felt in crushing the shell of this rebellion.

Garfield then went into a detailed discussion of the importance of a move
that would keep Bragg fully occupied and unable to reinforce Confederate
armies elsewhere. The problem was Rosecrans. "I write this with more sorrow than I can tell you, for I love every bone in his body, and next to my
desire to see the rebellion blasted, is my desire to see him blessed." But the
administration must demand action: "If the War Department has not always
been just, it has certainly been very indulgent to this Army. But I feel the
time has now come when it should allow no plea to keep this Army back
from the most vigorous activity."[2]

No loyal subordinate could write such a letter behind his commander's
back. But it is possible to sympathize with Garfield, whose anguish was so
apparent. Chase probably showed Garfield's letter to Stanton and others,
but eventually it became moot. In mid-August the Army of the Cumberland
was on the move, and on September 9 it captured Chattanooga.

For the Confederates, the situation in eastern Tennessee was now sufficiently desperate that the government in Richmond did something it had
never done before: it sent help from the Army of Northern Virginia. Over
the objections of Robert E. Lee, President Davis ordered Longstreet, with
two of his three divisions, to reinforce Bragg in Tennessee. With help on the
way, Bragg prepared to go on the offensive.

In Chattanooga, Rosecrans grew restive. No longer in touch with his ad-
versaries, he searched for passes through the mountains to the south. His
forces became badly dispersed but no attack came, and Rosecrans sought to
reassemble his army in some wooded country south of Chattanooga near
Chickamauga Creek. When Bragg attacked on September 19, the Army of
the Cumberland was ready.

The battle opened with a crushing attack on the Federal left. Although
the Army of the Cumberland gave way, Bragg had singled out the sector
defended by Gen. George H. Thomas, and in so doing had taken on one of
the most stubborn defensive fighters in the North. When fighting resumed

the next day, Bragg tried his luck elsewhere. Just before noon he sent Longstreet's corps against the Federal right.

Had Longstreet's attack come an hour earlier it would have encountered a strong defensive line. But it came shortly after one of Rosecrans's division commanders, Gen. Thomas J. Wood, had been ordered to pull out of the line to fill a supposed gap in the center. There was in fact no gap; the Federal troops responsible for that sector had concealed themselves in woods. But into the breach created by Rosecrans's order poured Longstreet's veterans.

Rosecrans attempted to rally his men, but he and his staff were swept to the rear in a torrent of men, horses, and wagons. The general, according to Garfield, "rode silently along, abstracted, as if he neither saw nor heard." Stunned, Rosecrans and a few of his staff retreated up the Dry Valley Road toward Rossville. Firing continued from the direction of Thomas's corps, and Garfield volunteered to find out what was going on. While Rosecrans retreated to Chattanooga, Garfield dashed to Thomas's headquarters to confirm that Thomas, the "Rock of Chickamauga," could continue to hold Horseshoe Ridge.

Thomas held, but Chickamauga was still a disaster for the Federals. It was time for Garfield to claim his congressional seat in Washington, and the young Ohioan was probably glad to be gone. Seeing off his subordinate, Rosecrans was his gracious self. The general order announcing Garfield's departure spoke of his intelligence, integrity, business capacity, and "thorough acquaintance with the wants of the army." The gruff Thomas, fearing for his commander's future, told Garfield, "You know the injustice of all these attacks on Rosecrans. Make it your business to set these matters straight."

Garfield did not see things quite the same way as Thomas did. He retained his affection for "Old Rosey," and in Congress would attempt to amend a resolution commending Thomas's actions at Chickamauga to include some mention of Rosecrans. But he was not about to become a last-ditch defender of a commander who had outworn his welcome with the Lincoln administration. Not only did he ignore Thomas's injunction to defend Rosecrans, but in private conversation he spoke critically of his erstwhile commander, much as he had written to Chase.

Considering Garfield's willingness to speak out, it is hardly surprising that rumors circulated in Washington that letters from Garfield to Chase had brought about Rosecrans's removal. Such stories were speculative, for it had been the defeat at Chickamauga that had assured Rosecrans's ouster. Lincoln and Stanton could put up with a great deal from victorious generals, and if Chickamauga had been a Federal victory, Rosecrans's position would have been secure.

The personal friendship between Garfield and Rosecrans might have continued had Rosecrans not entered politics, and as a Democrat at that. In

1880–the year in which Garfield was the Republican candidate for president–"Old Rosey" ran for Congress in California. During the campaign Garfield heard stories that Rosecrans had distributed some blatantly anti-Garfield campaign literature, and saw newspaper reports that quoted Rosecrans as calling him a thief. For his part, Rosecrans was angered by effusive campaign biographies that credited Garfield with all that had gone well with the Army of the Cumberland and blamed Rosecrans for all that had gone badly. "Old Rosey," never noted for his discretion, may have been provoked into making some harsh statements about his one-time subordinate.

Both Garfield and Rosecrans were successful in their campaigns. After the election Rosecrans wrote a friendly letter to Garfield, suggesting regret at some of his statements in the heat of the campaign and expressing the hope that "we stand on the old ground of cordial regard which existed before the election." The response was frigid. Garfield reminded Rosecrans of a statement in which he had said of Garfield that "many a young man had descended from honor to infamy." This was strong language, and Rosecrans was a bit presumptuous in assuming that Garfield would forgive and forget. The future president did neither. In a last letter to his old chief, Garfield characterized Rosecrans's campaign utterances as an insuperable barrier to friendly relations.

They never met again. In less than a year, Garfield, who had made his way "from log cabin to the White House," was dead from an assassin's bullet.

CHAPTER 10

The Night War Came to Portland, Maine

THE CONFEDERACY lost the Civil War, but in one campaign Confederate forces achieved every goal to which they could reasonably aspire. That campaign was the war on the high seas, waged against the Northern merchant marine by a handful of Confederate cruisers. A few Confederate warships, including several purchased in Britain, eventually burned or ransomed more than 200 Northern vessels—the maritime equivalent of Sherman's march through Georgia.

In earlier wars, commerce destroyers had attempted to send their prizes to a home port, where the ship would be sold and the proceeds credited to those responsible for the capture. In the Civil War, however, the Federal blockade made it virtually impossible to send prizes "home." As a result, the gray raiders usually destroyed those prizes that could be identified as enemy owned. When a U.S. ship was carrying neutral cargo, the Confederates usually made her skipper sign a ransom bond, obligating her owners to pay the value of the ship to Confederate authorities after the war.

One of the most feared of Confederate cruisers was the British-built *Florida*, initially commanded by the resourceful John Maffitt. For all her later success, the *Florida* for a time was a hard-luck ship. After taking on her ordnance in the Bahamas early in 1862, the ship was so ravaged by yellow fever that Maffitt took her through the Federal blockade into Mobile to recruit a new crew. Not until January 1863 was the *Florida* ready to return to sea, but once he had a crew Maffitt was again able to evade the Federal blockaders. In the course of two extended cruises, the *Florida* would eventually take 37 prizes.

Maffitt was always open to innovation, and when one of his junior officers came up with a proposal that they commission one of their prizes as a satellite raider, Maffitt was interested. On May 6, 1863, off San Roque, Brazil, the *Florida* had captured a Baltimore-based brig, the *Clarence*, with a load of cof-

Lt. Charles W. Read,
scourge of the New
England fishing fleet.
*U.S. Navy Imaging
Center*

fee. Now, one of Maffitt's young officers, Charles W. Read, had plans for
her, and he persuaded his captain that the investment of a few men in a
satellite raider would be a useful experiment.

Read, a 23-year-old Mississippian, was an Annapolis graduate, but not an
especially distinguished graduate, for he had graduated last in his class of 25
in 1860, earning the nickname "Savvy." Three years later, Read was unpre-
possessing in appearance, "little more than a boy, bright faced, alert . . .
rather slight, with a brown mustache."[1] But he had proved to be as audacious
at sea as the famous guerrilla leader John S. Mosby was on land.

After resigning his U.S. Navy commission in 1861, Read had distinguished himself in the unsuccessful Confederate defense of New Orleans. As
executive officer of the *McRae*, a merchant sloop that had been pressed into
service against Adm. David Farragut's fleet, Read took command of the craft
after her captain was fatally wounded in the Federal attack. Despite a fire in
the sail room, heavy loss of life, and the bursting of his pivot gun, Read had

saved the *McRae* and then taken over the CSS *Resolute*, a more powerful vessel that had been run ashore and abandoned by her commander. Read continued the fight in the *Resolute* and emerged as one of the few Confederate heroes in the New Orleans debacle.

Later, the combative Read had commanded a battery on the ironclad *Arkansas* in action against Federal gunboats on the Mississippi. After the *Arkansas* was destroyed to avoid capture, Read was detailed to the *Florida*, which had just run the blockade into Mobile. Maffitt, hearing of Read's exploits, requested that he be assigned to the *Florida*. When his ship finally returned to sea, Maffitt watched the young lieutenant closely, and his impressions were mixed. "Mr. Read is quiet and slow," Maffitt wrote in his journal, but he thought him "reliable and sure."[2]

Now, after only three months at sea, Read was asking for command of the captured *Clarence*, and for authority to conduct a strike into enemy-controlled waters off the Virginia coast. In Read's words,

> I propose to take the brig *Clarence* which we have just captured and with a crew of 20 men proceed to Hampton Roads and cut out a gunboat or steamer of the enemy.
>
> As I would be in possession of the brig's papers, and as the crew would not be large enough to excite suspicions, there can be no doubt of my passing Fort Monroe successfully. Once in the Roads I would be prepared to avail myself of any circumstances. . . . If it was found impossible to board a gunboat, or merchant steamer, it would be possible to fire the shipping at Baltimore.[3]

There doubtless had been some preliminary discussions between Maffitt and Read, for young Read took command of the *Clarence* on the very day of her capture. Maffitt indicated that Read might be able to cut out the *Sumpter*, a steamer believed to be anchored in an exposed position in Hampton Roads. Should this prove impossible, he might at least be able to surprise and burn some shipping in that crowded anchorage. But in giving Read command of the *Clarence*, Maffitt carefully avoided burdening him with instructions.

With or without orders, Read's was a high-risk enterprise. His only real weapon was a 12-pound gun, and apart from its cargo of coffee there were few supplies on the *Clarence*. Indeed, the absence of any prizes for a time threatened Read's mission. Then the *Clarence* fell in with a British merchantman who was happy to sell the Rebels some stores, especially when Read threw in 300 bags of coffee. The raider took its first prize on June 6, and followed it with captures on each of the next two days. But comments from the prisoners raised doubts as to the wisdom of a raid into Hampton Roads. According to the Yankees, security was extremely tight, and no vessels were allowed past Fortress Monroe except those carrying supplies for the Union forces.

Read—hopeful of finding a faster ship—kept all his options open. He altered course for the Virginia capes where, by flying a distress signal, he attracted the attention of a passing bark, the *Tacony*. Before *Tacony*'s master had an inkling that anything was amiss, Read led a boatload of men to the good Samaritan and seized his ship. A quick examination disclosed that the *Tacony* was a far better sailer than the *Clarence*, and Read transferred his crew to her.

While Read was exchanging ships, the schooner *Kate Stewart* arrived and moved in to investigate. Her arrival was awkward for Read, whose single cannon had not yet been installed on his new ship. But Read had installed some dummy guns on the *Clarence*, and now they proved their worth. Read trained them on the *Kate Stewart* and ordered her to heave to. The new arrival meekly complied, permitting Read to bond her and to use her as a conveyance for his prisoners. The unlamented *Clarence* was put to the torch.

By now Read had let his reddish mustache grow, and he resembled more an old-time buccaneer than an 1860 Annapolis graduate. Moving north up the coast, he captured the brig *Umpire*, carrying sugar and molasses from Cuba to Boston, on June 14. The *Umpire*—Read's seventh capture—was burned about 300 miles off the Delaware coast. Although his prizes generally were coastal vessels rather than the great clippers that were targeted by the *Alabama* and the *Florida*, the fact that Read was operating just offshore lent an immediacy to his activity. On June 14, Secretary of the Navy Gideon Welles sent a message to U.S. Navy commands in the major East Coast cities:

> It appears that the pirate *Clarence* have transferred themselves to the captured bark *Tacony* and have burned the *Clarence*. They have nothing but small arms. Charter or seize half a dozen moderate-sized, fast vessels; put on board an officer, a dozen men, plenty of small arms, and one or two howitzers. Send them out in various directions.[4]

Welles's order for ships to go in "various directions" was indicative of the confusion Read had sown. In any case, many of the small craft marshaled to chase the *Tacony* were inferior even to that lightly armed vessel. The Federals had no system to their pursuit, and only a vague idea of whom they were pursuing. On two occasions Read was hailed by vessels that were searching for the *Tacony*. When one Union warship hailed him to ask for news of the "pirate *Tacony*," Read responded through his speaking trumpet that he had seen her at dusk, pursuing an East Indiaman. He added a notional course, and watched the enemy head off on a wild goose chase.[5]

Read's log soon told of fresh captures:

On June 21 . . . captured and burned the clipper ship *Byzantium*, from London to New York, loaded with coal. On the same day burned the bark *Goodspeed*, from Londonderry to New York, in ballast.

On June 22 captured the fishing schooners *Marengo, Florence, Elizabeth Ann, Rufus Choate*, and *Ripple*. The *Florence* being an old vessel I bonded her and placed 75 prisoners on her. The other schooners were burned.

On June 24 . . . captured the ship *Shatemuc*, from Liverpool to Boston, with a large number of emigrants. I bonded her for $150,000. On the night of June 24 captured the fishing schooner *Archer*.[6]

All this Read accomplished through nerve and surprise, although he was greatly assisted by the Federals' inept pursuit. When the *Tacony*'s former master reached Philadelphia he told reporters of a great Confederate fleet, including the *Alabama* and the *Florida*, poised to devastate the Atlantic seaboard. In Washington, Welles was beside himself; he grumbled in his diary on June 23,

> None of our vessels have succeeded in capturing the Rebel pirate *Tacony*, which has committed great ravages along the coast, although I have sent out over 20 vessels in pursuit. Had she been promptly taken I should have been blamed for such a needless and expensive waste of strength; now I shall be censured for not doing more.[7]

Meanwhile, Read was considering how to make the secretary's task even more difficult. He continued to enjoy the advantage of surprise in sea lanes that the Federals considered their own. On June 20 he overhauled a liner, the *Isaac Webb*, carrying some 750 passengers, mostly immigrants bound for the New World. Read longed to burn the *Isaac Webb*, which was much his largest prize to date, but because he had no way of handling such a number of prisoners, he settled for a $40,000 ransom bond.

With the *Tacony* now the object of an intense search, Read was eager to change ships, preferably to a steamer. Once again, fortune favored the bold. On June 24 he captured a fast schooner, the *Archer*, and soon had his crew and his much-traveled 12-pounder on board. His new command was not a steamer, but Read was pleased nevertheless: "The schooner *Archer* is a fishing vessel of 90 tons, sails well, and is easily handled. No Yankee gunboat would even dream of suspecting us. I therefore think we will dodge our pursuers for a short time."[8] To further confuse his pursuers, Read burned the *Tacony*. Let the Yankees chase a nonexistent ship!

Read's depredations, so close to shore, caused panic along the Atlantic seaboard. Shippers bombarded the Lincoln administration with demands for protection and for improved harbor defenses. One group demanded that warships be stationed at the Grand Banks for the entire fishing season, noting that in the absence of such protection the entire fishing fleet was at risk. Whereas most of the ships burned on the high seas by the Confederates were insured and many were jointly owned, this was rarely the case with the New England fishing fleet. The loss of a boat was disastrous for the owner, and the political repercussions were immediate. Welles complained to his diary on July 22, "There is quite a panic along the entire New England coast. It is quite impossible to furnish all the vessels desired, and there is consequently the disagreeable result of refusal."[9]

The gloomy Welles had a streak of stubborn integrity, and he stoutly resisted demands from the merchants of New York and Boston for ironclads to be stationed in their ports for defense. But he failed to consider stationing a ship or two on the major fishing grounds, to protect the fishing boats that were Read's immediate target. Instead, he continued to send warships to wherever the *Tacony* or some other raider was last reported.

Meanwhile, Read, in the *Archer*, was contemplating the most audacious stroke of all, an attack on an enemy harbor. The morning of June 26 saw the *Archer* off Portland, Maine, her crew in scruffy fishermen's garb and their vessel indistinguishable from any other fishing schooner. Read picked up a dory with two lobstermen who, when told they were prisoners of the Confederate navy, at first thought the whole thing a great joke. After a hot breakfast they accepted their lot and cheerfully told what they knew of security in Portland harbor. The port was defended, they said, by a revenue cutter, the *Caleb Cushing*, and the *Chesapeake*, a passenger steamer operating between Portland and New York City.

That evening the *Archer*, guided by the gregarious lobstermen, made her way past the guns of Fort Preble into the harbor of Portland. At the last moment Read briefed his officers on his plan. They would capture the *Chesapeake*, burn such shipping in the harbor as they could manage, and then take the *Chesapeake* to sea. Not all of Read's officers cared for the plan. His engineer, Eugene Browne, doubted whether he could handle the *Chesapeake*'s engines without assistance. He also suspected that the steamer's boilers would be cold, making a speedy getaway impossible.

Faced with these misgivings, another commander might have scuttled the entire project. Not Charles Read. He did switch targets, however, deciding to seize the *Caleb Cushing*, after Browne expressed confidence that he could handle her engines. As night fell, Read led a prayer, calling on the Almighty to bless their enterprise and to bring independence to the Confederacy. Then he moved the *Archer* to just outside the Portland harbor. At about 1:30 A.M. on June 27, Read and 19 others, in two boats, rowed with muffled oars for the *Caleb Cushing*.[10] Once he had seized the cutter, he would see what damage he could do in the harbor.

Read's offshore captures notwithstanding, the war seemed far away to residents of Portland, Maine. Had it not been for the casualty lists from Virginia, there might have been no war at all. And a factor unknown to Read was now working in his favor; the skipper of the *Caleb Cushing* had died and his replacement was not yet on board. The acting commander was a young lieutenant, Dudley Davenport, and half of the *Cushing*'s crew were enjoying liberty ashore, for the cutter was scheduled to go to sea shortly, in pursuit of the elusive *Tacony*.

In the predawn's half-light, two men on the *Cushing*'s watch spotted the boats from *Tacony* and reported to Davenport in his cabin. By the time the three men had returned to the deck, however, the Confederates were scrambling over the rails. Read himself covered the three Federals with his pistol, promising that he would shoot if they uttered a sound. His comrades went below and captured the cutter's crew while most were still in their hammocks.

Thus far, all had gone according to Read's amended plan. But by the time he had secured his prize, the offshore breeze had died and the tide had begun to come in. Read had no time to burn shipping in the harbor and, in a weak breeze, would do well to reach the open sea.

Once again, the young Mississippian improvised. While Browne sought to work up steam in an unfamiliar engine room, Read used his two boats to tow the cutter. It was heavy rowing against the tide, and at dawn the *Caleb Cushing* was still within range of the guns of Fort Preble. Then a fresh breeze rose, and by midmorning the cutter had steam up and was out of range of the fort. Read recognized the chastened Davenport as an Annapolis classmate, and invited him to join in a hot breakfast.

Ashore, meanwhile, people were noticing that the *Caleb Cushing* had departed ahead of schedule. Church bells tolled the alarm, and residents poured into the streets. Davenport was a Southerner by birth, and rumor had it that he was somehow behind his ship's premature departure. The collector of the port, Jedediah Jewett, organized a pursuit; he commandeered a passenger vessel, the *Forest City*, and piled on board those of the *Cushing*'s liberty crew that he could find, plus 30 soldiers from Fort Preble. The mayor of Portland, Jacob McLellan, similarly commandeered the *Chesapeake*, the fast steamer that had been Read's initial target. When a representative of the New York Line protested against his vessel's being turned into a warship, McLellan delayed only long enough to protect the ship's engines with bales of cotton.

Read's bold venture was now in serious jeopardy. Thanks largely to Jewett, the Federal pursuit was prompt and, involving two steamers as it did, was likely to prove successful. By 11:00 A.M. the *Forest City* had approached within two miles of the *Caleb Cushing*, and Read opened fire with the cutter's

32-pounder. His shots were sufficiently close that Jewett chose to lag back until the *Chesapeake* came up. With the arrival of the larger vessel, the two skippers, using speaking trumpets, agreed on a strategy. They would approach the *Cushing* from opposite sides and attempt to ram her.

Meanwhile, Read had a problem. Except for a few shot on a rack near the gun, there appeared to be no ammunition for the cutter's 32-pounder. Davenport told him that the *Caleb Cushing* was just off the ways and had not yet taken aboard her normal ordnance. As a result, when the *Forest City* and the *Chesapeake* returned to the attack, Read knew that the game was up. He did not go quietly, however. In a final gesture of defiance, he fired hunks of a great cheese brought up from the galley—leading one Yankee on board the *Chesapeake* to remark that the pirates were firing "stinkpots at us, like the Chinese."[11] After loading his crew and his prisoners into two boats, Read torched the *Caleb Cushing* fore and aft. Thirty minutes later the fire reached her magazines, and the cutter exploded in a ball of flame.

Could Davenport have deceived his Annapolis classmate in saying that the *Cushing* was largely unarmed?

While Read and his crew were taken prisoner, the *Archer* attempted to sneak back to sea. She looked like any other fishing schooner and might have escaped with her skeleton crew had it not been for one of the lobstermen who had been so helpful to the Confederates. Perhaps angered at having been put into irons by his captors, he called attention to the *Archer*, which was quickly overtaken and captured.

The Portland gentry did not take kindly to Read's type of warfare. For down-easters, it was bad enough when Confederate cruisers burned Northern clippers on the high seas; for the Rebels to destroy fishing boats—the sole source of a livelihood for their owners—passed the bounds of civilized warfare. While being marched to jail, Read and his men were harassed in the streets, and their clothes left in tatters. The Confederates eventually spent a year in Boston's Fort Warren before being exchanged. Read himself briefly commanded a Confederate ironclad in the final months of the war.

He and his crew had captured 22 prizes in just 21 days, demonstrating how even a small raider could inflict severe damage on an unprotected concentration of coastal craft. Read accomplished this feat without any loss of life, managing to stir up considerable hysteria along the New England coast at the very time that Lee was marching towards Gettysburg. But in his destruction of fishing craft, Read was operating on the edge of the accepted laws of war. The U.S. Supreme Court would later rule, in a case unrelated to the Civil War, that coastal fishing vessels "unarmed and honestly pursuing their peaceful calling of catching and bringing in fresh fish" were exempt from capture as prizes of war."[12]

And there is the matter of Read's raid into Portland harbor. The young Confederate might be excused for assuming that the *Caleb Cushing* would be carrying a normal quota of powder and shot, but even if she had been fully armed, Read could not have escaped two Yankee steamers. Having successfully eluded a score of Navy pursuers and desiring to continue his cruise in something more imposing than the *Archer*, the gallant Read fell victim to overconfidence.

Months later, hearing of Read's exploits, John Maffitt wrote in his journal that his erstwhile protégé was "daring beyond the point of martial prudence."[13] The skipper of the *Florida* may have had the last word on "Savvy" Read.

CHAPTER 11

▬

Representative Recruit for Abraham Lincoln

THE WAR was going better than many Northerners realized. By mid-1864 the Federals had been in control of the Mississippi for more than a year, the Army of Northern Virginia was fully occupied keeping Grant away from Richmond, and Sherman was about to embark on his destructive March to the Sea. But from the perspective of the Lincoln administration in Washington, the trend of the war still left much to be desired.

The end was not in sight, and the appalling casualties being inflicted on Grant's army before Richmond raised the real possibility that the administration would be defeated in the November elections. Although earlier draft calls had prompted a surge of volunteers—volunteers received enlistment bonuses, whereas draftees did not—the North's third draft call, announced on July 18, 1864, had prompted only a trickle of enlistments.

As a result, the ranks of the Federal armies were being filled by conscription, and among the conscripts more than half were substitutes. The system under which a draftee could hire a substitute for $300 or more was hardly egalitarian—a parody on a patriotic song ran, "We Are Coming Father Abraham, Three Hundred Dollars More." Nevertheless, the hiring of substitutes was an accepted practice in Europe and had been commonplace in America during the Revolution.

When the first conscription legislation was passed in March 1863, substitutes had been widely available at the "going" price of $300. One year later, however, able-bodied men could name their own price. The booming Northern economy had shrunk the pool of unemployed men to the vanishing point, and the grim realities of army life discouraged volunteers.

As commander in chief, President Lincoln was in no danger of being drafted and handed a rifle. Given the poor response to the July 1864 draft call, however, the president appears to have decided that his example in providing a recruit might remove some of the stigma associated with hiring sub-stitutes and encourage other men of means to do likewise.

On September 30 Lincoln told Provost Marshal General James B. Fry of his desire to finance a substitute, and asked him to find a suitable candidate. Given the shortage of able-bodied men this was no easy task, and there was also a question of character. It would hardly do for the president's "represen-tative recruit" to be an alcoholic or a deserter. In pursuit of Lincoln's instruc-tion, Fry gave the job of finding a substitute to Noble D. Larner, a District of Columbia resident who knew the president and who was in charge of re-cruiting in the city's third ward.

Undeterred by the manpower shortage, Larner found his man overnight. As reported in the *Washington Star*,

> Mr. Larner set to work to procure as fine and healthy looking recruit as he could, and today secured a young man, twenty years of age, named John Summerfield Staples, from Stroudsburg, Mon-roe County, Pennsylvania. . . . Staples is not so tall as the Presi-dent, but is well formed, stout and healthy, and there is every indication that he will prove an excellent soldier.

Staples was no stranger to the army. He had enlisted in the Pennsylvania militia in November 1862, and, after what must have been very rudimentary training, had accompanied his regiment to North Carolina, where Gen. Ambrose E. Burnside was conducting operations along the Carolina coast. In January 1863 Staples contracted typhoid fever and was hospitalized at New Bern until May 5, when he was discharged on a surgeon's certificate. He later moved to Washington and was working there as a carpenter when Larner approached him with his unusual proposal. If Staples was not an extraordinary catch in terms of his health, he was at least available, and the fact that his father was a Methodist minister doubtless constituted evidence of good character.

On October 1, General Fry, accompanied by Larner, John Staples, and John's father, called on President Lincoln. According to one account, Gen-eral Fry performed the introductions, telling the president, "This is the man who is to represent you in the army for the next year." Lincoln commented favorably on Staples's appearance and health, saying that he believed Staples would do his duty. Larner presented the president with a framed certificate to the effect that he had financed a "representative recruit." Lincoln then authorized Fry to draw on his bank for a recruiting bonus of $500. The president expressed a hope that good fortune would accompany Staples in his military service, and his visitors withdrew.

Private Staples's tour of duty as the president's substitute proved unevent-ful. He was attached to the 2nd District of Columbia Regiment and served first as a clerk at Camp Sedgewick, in Alexandria, Virginia. Later he worked

Enlistment certificate for John S. Staples, Lincoln's substitute in the Union army.
National Archives

in a regimental hospital. There must have been many jocular remarks about
not allowing anything to happen to Mr. Lincoln's recruit, but the record does
not indicate that Staples received special treatment. He was mustered out on
September 12, 1865, three months ahead of schedule.

Staples returned to Stroudsburg after the war. There he married, fathered
a daughter, and worked as a wheelwright. He later moved to Waterloo, New
York. When his eyesight began to fail he filed for a disability pension, but his
request was denied on the grounds that the disability was unrelated to his
military service. John Staples died in 1888 at the age of 43, his curious war
history largely forgotten.

CHAPTER 12

The Fiery Trail
of the *Alabama*

WORKERS IN the John Laird Shipyard at Birkenhead, near Liverpool, watched attentively on the morning of May 15, 1862, as a handsome steam bark slid into the waters of the Mersey River. The vessel was known to them as No. 290, for hers was the 290th keel laid at the Laird yards. Upon launching, she was named the *Enrica*, but the identity of her owners remained a subject of speculation, for she was being built to the specifications of a Royal Navy cruiser. As May turned into June, the new vessel sprouted three tall masts that would enable her to carry a broad spread of canvas, and took on two 300-horsepower engines for steam propulsion.

In the waterfront bars of Liverpool, it was said with a wink that the actual purchaser of the *Enrica* was the Southern Confederacy, then locked in a war to establish its independence from the United States. For once, the tipsters were right on the mark. The possibility that No. 290 was destined for the Confederacy had not been lost on the U.S. minister in London, Charles Francis Adams, who was bombarding the Foreign Office with demands that the ship be seized. By mid-July, James Bulloch, the adroit Confederate naval agent who had supervised construction of the *Enrica* for the government in Richmond, knew that time was growing short.

The ever-imaginative Bulloch arranged for the *Enrica*'s departure from England in the guise of a gala trial run. On the fine morning of July 29, the new bark sailed down the Mersey with local dignitaries on board. At dusk, however, Bulloch and his guests returned to Liverpool on a tugboat, leaving the *Enrica* off the coast of Wales at Moelfra Bay. British authorities had in fact been attempting to detain the *Enrica*, and Bulloch had thwarted them by the narrowest of margins.

On Sunday, August 10, the *Enrica* arrived at the island of Terceira in the Azores. Eight days later the *Agrippina*, a tender under charter to Bulloch, showed up with equipment for the Confederate cruiser, including a 100-

pound Blakely rifle, an 8-inch smoothbore, six 32-pounders, and provisions. That afternoon a second vessel, the *Bahama,* arrived with officers and hands for the new vessel. Thanks to Bulloch, the complicated logistics of equipping and manning a cruiser outside British waters were carried out without a hitch. On Sunday, August 24, in the presence of the crews of the *Enrica* and the *Bahama,* the Union Jack fluttered down from the mainmast and was replaced by the naval ensign of the Confederacy. A band played "Dixie," and the mystery ship was officially christened the Confederate steamer *Alabama.*

The cruiser's designated commander was 52-year-old Raphael Semmes, a Maryland native who had taken up residence in Alabama. Semmes had entered the U.S. Navy in 1832 and by 1861 had achieved the rank of commander. He was widely read in naval history and marine law and had written several books, including a lively narrative of his naval service during the Mexican War. A strong advocate of states' rights, Semmes had resigned his Federal commission even before the firing on Fort Sumter.

In April 1861, Confederate Secretary of the Navy Stephen Mallory gave Semmes command of one of the South's first warships, the 437-ton screw steamer *Sumter.* The *Sumter* and her more powerful successors were intended to tackle one of two missions that Mallory had established for the Confederate navy: to attack the North's merchant marine, so as to increase the cost of the war to the enemy and thus encourage Lincoln to acknowledge Southern independence. The navy's other mission—to construct a fleet of ironclads capable of breaking the Federal blockade—was beyond Confederate capabilities, but the first was not.

It had taken Semmes about two months to convert the *Sumter* into a warship, but he assembled a nucleus of able officers. The *Sumter* broke the Federal blockade off New Orleans on June 30, 1861, and reached the open sea. Thereafter, during a six-month cruise, the little raider burned 8 Northern ships and released 10 others on bond—a procedure under which the owners of an American ship's neutral cargo were expected to reimburse the Confederacy for goods not destroyed.

Eventually, boiler problems and a need for coal obliged the *Sumter* to call at Gibraltar, where she was blockaded by three Federal warships, with no prospect of escape. Having made the most of his ship's limited capabilities, Semmes ordered the sale of the *Sumter* and set out for Britain with most of his officers. There, to the disappointment of Bulloch, who had hoped for the command, Semmes was given the far more powerful *Alabama.*

Semmes's first challenge in the Azores was to persuade enough British sailors to sign aboard the *Alabama* so that he could take his new command to sea. He assured the hands of the *Alabama* and the *Bahama* that they were free to return to Britain if they chose, but he painted a glowing picture of life aboard the *Alabama.* He offered good pay—£4 10s. a month in gold for seamen, and £7 for firemen—plus grog twice a day and the prospect of prize money. He touched only briefly on the issues of the American war but promised excitement and adventure. To his relief, he was able to sign on 80 British crewmen—enough to take the *Alabama* to sea. As time went on, he would supplement this nucleus with recruits from captured vessels.

Once Semmes had his officers and crew, he turned his attention to his ship. The *Alabama* represented the zenith of a hybrid marine form: ships powered by both sail and steam. She measured 220 feet in length, had a beam of 32 feet, and displaced 1,040 tons. She carried enough coal for 18 days' steaming and had an innovation found on few ships of her day—a condenser that provided a gallon of fresh water per day for each man on board, enabling her to remain at sea for extended periods. Her two-bladed screw could be raised into a well when she was under sail, thus posing no drag in the water. She could make about 12 knots under sail alone, to which her engines could add another 3 knots. She came with a year's supply of spare gear. In the words of one of her officers, Lt. Arthur Sinclair, the *Alabama* "was at the same time a perfect steamer and a perfect sailing vessel, each entirely independent of the other." The ship's armament also was impressive: six 32-pounders and two pivot guns. A visitor to the *Alabama* would comment, "What strikes one most . . . is to see so small a vessel carrying such large metal."

Semmes was under orders to avoid engagements with enemy warships, for his was a special mission. The *Alabama*, as her commander wrote later, was the first steamship in the history of the world, the defective little *Sumter* excepted, that was let loose against the commerce of a great commercial people." And Semmes set to his mission with a vengeance.

The *Alabama* had been at sea for only 10 days when, on September 5, she sighted the first of the 65 victims she would claim over the next 22 months. The ship was a whaler—the *Ocmulgee*, of Edgartown, Massachusetts—and the capture was easy, for the *Ocmulgee* had a whale lashed alongside when the *Alabama* approached. The raider had been flying the American flag, an accepted ruse in war, and, in Semmes's recollection, nothing could exceed the Yankee skipper's "blank stare of astonishment" when the *Alabama* at length ran up the Confederate ensign.

The *Ocmulgee*'s crew was transferred to the *Alabama*, along with some provisions; officers were permitted to bring one trunk with them, others a single bag. Semmes prepared to burn the whaler, but with the guile that would become his trademark, he waited until daylight: Whalers operated in clusters, and he did not want to scatter them with an unexplained fire at night.

The *Alabama* spent two months in the Azores, burning eight vessels in all. The American whaling fleet, or what was left of it, returned to its home ports in New England, where shipowners filled the Northern press with tales of the "pirate" Semmes. The *Alabama*, too, worked her way westward. Semmes briefly considered throwing a few shells into New York City, but he thought better of it and instead seized several grain carriers off the Newfoundland banks.

The *Alabama*'s captures followed a pattern. The raider would hail a ship on sight. If she did not heave to, Semmes would fire a blank cartridge. If she still failed to respond, he would send a shot from a 32-pounder across her bow, and that would bring her to a halt. While the prize was boarded, Semmes stayed in his cabin; the skipper of his victim was taken to him there. Any ship whose papers showed her to be of neutral ownership was released. If she was U.S.–owned, Semmes transferred her crew to the *Alabama* and torched the ship.

For a commerce raider, the *Alabama* operated under an unusual handicap: Because of the Federal blockade, she had no home port to which Semmes might send prizes. He thus had to burn most of the ships he captured. After appropriating any usable provisions, a Rebel boarding party would pile up furniture and mattresses, douse them with lard or some other flammable substance, and fire the ship. Semmes's first officer was another veteran of the Old Navy, John McIntosh Kell. The tough, red-bearded Kell later wrote: "To watch the leaping flames on a burning ship gives an indescribable mental excitement that did not decrease with the frequency of the light, but it was always a relief to know the ships were tenantless as they disappeared in the lonely grandeur, specks of vanishing light in the 'cradle of the deep.' "

Between captures, the crew had ample opportunity to take the measure of their skipper. Semmes had just turned 53 and was not physically imposing; some thought him past his prime for sea command. His one idiosyncrasy was a carefully cultivated mustache that led his sailors to call him Old Beeswax. He was a tough disciplinarian and in his postwar memoir he outlined his command philosophy:

> On week days . . . about one fourth of the crew was exercised, either at the battery or with small arms. This not only gave them efficiency in the use of their weapons, but kept them employed— the constant employment of my men being a fundamental article of my philosophy. . . . My crew were never so happy as when they had plenty to do, and but little to think about.

Whatever the hands may have thought of Old Beeswax, Semmes appears to have enjoyed the respect of virtually all his officers. First Officer Kell worshiped his commander. And Lieutenant Sinclair later wrote that "Semmes [understood] just how to keep himself near the hearts and in the confidence of his men, without in the slightest degree descending from his dignity, or permitting direct approach." Semmes also impressed everyone with his professionalism. He was a student of every facet of seamanship—he digresses in his memoir to discuss how variations in temperature affect the currents—and he had a childlike wonder at the natural beauty of the sea.

A fierce-looking
Raphael Semmes—
"Old Beeswax" as
his sailors called
him—posed for this
photo in 1863.
Library of Congress

Probably only Kell glimpsed the virulent hatred that Semmes nourished for his enemy, the Yankees. Of them Semmes had written in his journal, "A people so devoid of Christian charity, and wanting in so many of the essentials of honesty, cannot be abandoned to their own folly by a just and benevolent God." Yet not even his loathing for Northerners as a class could totally destroy his admiration for them as seamen, and as the war went on, the task of burning their ships became less satisfying to him.

Semmes dealt with his prisoners as humanely as conditions permitted. Captured crews were usually housed on deck but were afforded some protection from the elements. When the prisoners included women passengers, Semmes's officers turned over the wardroom for their use. Prisoners received full rations, and cooks among their number had access to the *Alabama*'s galley. Officers were occasionally placed in irons, generally after

Semmes had heard reports of mistreatment of Confederate prisoners. Because prisoners were a nuisance, Semmes got rid of them as fast as possible. Sometimes he landed them at a neutral port, but more often he transferred them to a captured ship whose cargo he had bonded.

From Newfoundland the raider worked her way south to Martinique, where, on their first liberty, crewmen got so drunk that Semmes put some 20 sailors in irons. The incident was a reminder that while the *Alabama*'s officers were reliable seamen, committed to the Confederate cause, most of the British crewmen were not. Much as the duke of Wellington once called his army the scum of the earth, Semmes called his crew "a precious set of rascals . . . faithless in . . . contracts, liars, thieves, and drunkards. There are . . . exceptions to this rule, but I am ashamed to say of the sailor class of the present day that I believe my crew to be a fair representation of it."

Kell, who supervised the boarding of every prize, had a firm rule that no member of the *Alabama*'s crew could board a captured vessel until any supply of spirits was thrown overboard. Even so, he and Semmes were constantly on the alert for smuggled liquor.

Semmes had passed up the temptation to show his flag off New York City the previous fall, but in the Caribbean he was inclined to stretch his orders and play a role in the ground campaign along the Texas coast. A Federal force under Gen. Nathaniel P. Banks had captured Galveston in October 1862. Confederate forces had subsequently recaptured Galveston, but the city was blockaded by five Federal warships when the black-hulled *Alabama* arrived there on January 11, 1863.

Semmes considered his options. The city that he had contemplated bombarding was now in friendly hands, and he could hardly take on five enemy warships. While he deliberated, the Federals detached one of their fleet, the gunboat *Hatteras*, to investigate the new arrival. It was a fatal error. Semmes set out toward open water, steaming slowly, luring his pursuer away from the other Federal warships.

Night had fallen by the time the *Hatteras* reached shouting distance of the *Alabama*, and Semmes, in reply to a hail from the Yankee, identified his ship as the HMS *Petrel*. While the Federal captain dispatched a boat to check out his story, Semmes ran up the Confederate ensign and loosed a broadside at point-blank range.

The *Hatteras* was an underpowered side-wheeler that had no business engaging the powerful *Alabama*. The U.S. gunboat struck her flag after an exchange that lasted only 13 minutes; a few minutes later she sank in the shallow waters of the gulf. Two of her crew had been killed and three wounded. Semmes rescued the survivors and set course for the Atlantic.

The *Alabama* stopped at Jamaica, where Semmes paroled his prisoners and partook of the hospitality that he would encounter in British possessions throughout the *Alabama*'s two-year cruise. Then he turned his ship southeast around Brazil to work the heavily traveled trade routes of the South Atlantic. Four more ships were stopped and burned in the first weeks of 1863, raising the *Alabama*'s total to 30.

Coaling the raider was proving to be a problem. She still had the services of a tender, the *Agrippina*, but it was difficult for Semmes to anticipate every supply requirement and he had little confidence in the master of the *Agrippina*. In southern latitudes, moreover, coal tended to be scarce as well as expensive. Fortunately for Semmes, he had a generous supply of gold for payment of ship's bills in remote corners of the world.

In June 1863, off the coast of South America, Semmes captured the U.S. clipper *Conrad*, bound for New York with wool from Argentina. He had been waiting for such a prize, and, rather than burning her, he commissioned her as a Confederate cruiser, the *Tuscaloosa*, arming her with guns captured from another ship. This was one more example of Semmes's creative approach to commerce raiding, but the *Tuscaloosa* had little success as a raider.

From South America Semmes set sail for the Cape of Good Hope. In August 1863 the *Alabama* reached Cape Town, where Semmes supervised some badly needed repairs on his ship. The Confederate commander found himself a celebrity in the British colony, in part because his latest seizure—the *Sea Bride*, from Boston—had been within sight of the cape. As in Jamaica, the *Alabama*'s officers were exhaustively entertained. Semmes held a shipboard "open house" that produced, in his view, "a generous outpouring of the better classes." He also came within a day of encountering a Federal warship that had been dogging his trail, a well-armed paddle-wheeler, the *Vanderbilt*.

For all the outrage in the Northern press about the *Alabama*'s depredations, pursuit of the raider was disorganized and ineffectual. This was partly deliberate. The Confederacy never had more than a handful of commerce raiders at sea, and of these only the *Florida*—commissioned about the same time as the *Alabama* and destined to destroy 38 ships—was in the *Alabama*'s class. The Lincoln administration regarded the maintenance and strengthening of the blockade of Southern ports as its first priority; it was not willing to weaken the blockade to track down the *Alabama,* the *Florida,* or one of their lesser consorts.

Even making allowances, however, Federal pursuit of the *Alabama* showed little imagination. The U.S. Navy dogged Semmes's trail as if convinced that the raider would remain in the area of its most recent capture. Semmes later wrote that had Secretary of the Navy Gideon Welles stationed a heavier and faster ship than the *Alabama* along two or three of the most traveled sea-lanes, "he must have driven me off, or greatly crippled me in my movements."

From Cape Town the *Alabama* worked her way eastward across the Indian Ocean. There, most of the ships encountered proved to be neutral, and friendly captains warned Semmes that the Federals had a warship, the *Wyo-*

ming, patrolling the Sunda Strait between Sumatra and Java. Nevertheless, Semmes seized and burned a New York clipper, the *Winged Racer*, off Java, and set off in pursuit of another, the *Contest*, the next morning.

The pursuit of the *Contest* proved to be an omen. For the first time, the *Alabama*, employing both sail and steam, was initially unable to overtake her prey. But the sun rose higher, the morning breeze died, and the Confederate raider eventually closed in. The *Contest* was burned—not without regret, for several of the *Alabama*'s officers vowed that they had never seen a more beautiful vessel. Only the failing wind had enabled the *Alabama* to make the capture, however, and Semmes realized that 18 months at sea had taken a toll on his ship.

On December 21, 1863, the *Alabama* anchored at Singapore, where Semmes saw new evidence of the effectiveness of his campaign: Singapore harbor was filled with U.S. ships that had taken refuge there rather than chance an encounter with the *Alabama*. Within days of her arrival, about half of these were sold to neutral nations and flew new flags. The *Straits Times* estimated that Singapore was playing host to 17 American vessels aggregating 12,000 tons, some of which had been there for upwards of three months.

On Christmas Eve, 1863, the *Alabama* set course westward. Pickings were predictably slim, but the crew had their hands full with their own ship. The raider's boilers were operating at reduced efficiency, and some of her timbers were split beyond repair. First Officer Kell observed that the *Alabama* was "loose at every joint, her seams were open, and the copper on her bottom was in rolls." For all of Semmes's skill and improvisation, nothing but a month in dry dock could restore the raider to fighting trim.

By early March the *Alabama* was again off Cape Town, but because a belligerent vessel could provision at the same neutral port only once in a three-month period, she had to pass 10 days offshore before docking. After coaling at Cape Town, Semmes turned northward. He intended to put his ship into dry dock in France, but he must have realized that the time necessary for repairs made it likely that the *Alabama* would be blockaded in port as the *Sumter* had been.

On April 22 the raider made the second of only three captures during 1864, the *Rockingham*, carrying a cargo of guano from Peru to Ireland. After the crew was taken off, Semmes directed that the prize be used for target practice—the raider's first live gun drill in many months. Sinclair later recalled that the sea was smooth and that the gun crews "amused themselves blithely" at point-blank range. Semmes thought his gun crews fired "to good effect," but Kell was less impressed: Of 24 rounds fired, only 7 were seen to inflict damage. Ultimately, Semmes had to burn the *Rockingham*.

On April 27 the *Alabama* made her final capture, the *Tycoon*, out of New York with a mixed cargo. Semmes burned the Yankee vessel and resumed his northward course. He later wrote:

The poor old *Alabama* was . . . like the wearied fox-hound, limping back after a long chase. . . . Her commander, like herself, was well-nigh worn down. Vigils by night and by day . . . had laid, in the three years of war he had been afloat, a load of a dozen years on his shoulders. The shadows of a sorrowful future, too, began to rest upon his spirit. The last batch of newspapers captured were full of disasters. Might it not be that, after all our trials and sacrifices, the cause for which we were struggling would be lost?

On June 11, 1864, the *Alabama* docked at the French port of Cherbourg. Word of her arrival was telegraphed all over Europe, and three days later the U.S. Navy ship *Kearsarge* appeared off the breakwater. Semmes had not yet received permission to make repairs at the French navy docks at Cherbourg, but he was allowed to disembark his prisoners and take on coal.

The Confederate commander faced a crucial decision. He knew that his ship needed a refit, and he probably realized that the prudent course would be to do as he had with the *Sumter*: put her up for sale and fight another day. But his fighting blood was up, and he had no great respect for his enemies. Nor was he inclined to solicit recommendations from his officers; as skipper of the *Sumter* and then of the *Alabama*, he was accustomed to making his own decisions. Shortly after the *Kearsarge* appeared, he called Kell to his cabin and explained his intentions:

As you know, the arrival of the *Alabama* at this port has been tele-graphed to all parts of Europe. Within a few days, Cherbourg will be effectively blockaded by Yankee cruisers. It is uncertain whether or not we shall be permitted to repair the *Alabama* here, and in the meantime, the delay is to our advantage. I think we may whip the *Kearsarge*, the two vessels being of wood and carrying about the same number of men and guns. Besides, Mr. Kell, although the Confederate States government has ordered me to avoid engagements with the enemy's cruisers, I am tired of running from that flaunting rag!

Kell was not sure the decision to fight was wise. He reminded Semmes that in the *Rockingham* gun drill only one in three fuses had seemed effective. But Semmes was not to be deterred. He sent a message to Capt. John A. Winslow of the *Kearsarge*, whom he had known in the Old Navy: He intended to fight.

Sunday, June 19, 1864, was a bright, cloudless day off Cherbourg. Aboard the *Alabama*, boilers were fired at daybreak, and Semmes inspected his crew at muster. Decks and brasswork were immaculate, and the crewmen were dressed in blue trousers and white tops. By 9:45 the cruiser was under way, cheered on by the crews of two French warships in the harbor.

The clash between the *Alabama* and the *Kearsarge* was, among other things, pure theater. It seemed that everyone in France wanted to watch what would prove to be the last one-on-one duel of the era of wooden ships. Excursion trains brought the curious, and throngs of small craft hovered outside the breakwater. Painter Edouard Manet, with brushes, paints, and easel, was on one of them.

The two ships were almost equal in size and armament. Both were hybrid steamers of about the same tonnage. The *Alabama* carried 149 crewmen and mounted eight guns; the *Kearsarge* had a crew of 163 and mounted seven guns. The outcome of the battle would depend largely on the skill of the gun crews and the condition of the ships, but the *Kearsarge* had an ace in the hole: The enterprising Winslow had made imaginative use of his ship's chains, draping them along vulnerable parts of the hull as impromptu armor and concealing them behind wood paneling. Semmes later denied knowing of the chains, but there is evidence that he was warned about them.

After the *Alabama* entered the English Channel, Semmes steered directly for his antagonist, some four miles away. He rotated his two pivot guns to starboard and prepared to engage the enemy on that side. The *Alabama* opened fire at about 11 A.M., and soon both ships were exchanging shots from their starboard batteries. The *Kearsarge* sought to run under the *Alabama*'s stern, but Semmes parried this move by turning to starboard.

The two antagonists thus fought on a circular track, much of the time at a range of about 500 yards. They made seven complete circles during the course of the action, reminding one Northern sailor of "two flies crawling around on the rim of a saucer." Semmes may initially have wanted to put his ship alongside the *Kearsarge* for boarding, but the Yankee's greater speed ruled out this option.

From the first, the firing from the *Alabama* was rapid and wild. The Confederate cruiser fired more than 300 rounds, only 28 of which struck the *Kearsarge*, many of them in the rigging. In their excitement the *Alabama*'s gunners fired some shot without removing the caps on their fuses, preventing them from exploding, and in other cases fired ramrods as well. It was not a disciplined performance. One of the *Alabama*'s crew conceded that the Confederate batteries were badly served: "The men all fought well, but the gunners did not know how to point and elevate the guns." In addition, the dark smoke emitted by the *Alabama*'s guns lent credence to Kell's fear that the raider's powder had deteriorated.

In contrast, Winslow and his crew fought with disciplined professionalism. "The firing now became very hot," Semmes later related," and . . . soon began to tell upon our hull, knocking down, killing and disabling a number of men . . . in different parts of the ship." Semmes ordered his gunners to use solid shot as well as shell, but to no effect. Meanwhile, the *Alabama*'s rudder was destroyed, forcing the Confederates to steer with tackles. In desperation,

Semmes offered a reward to anyone who could put the *Kearsarge*'s forward pivot gun out of action. Sinclair recalled how an 11-inch shell from that weapon entered the *Alabama* at the waterline and exploded in the engine room, "in its passage throwing a volume of water on board, hiding for a moment the guns of [my] division." With his fires out, Semmes attempted to steer for land, only to have the *Kearsarge* station herself between the *Alabama* and the coast.

Shortly after noon Semmes gave the order to abandon ship. The *Alabama* had suffered only 9 killed in the battle, but some 20 others, including Semmes, had been wounded; 12 more would be drowned. Semmes and Kell,

A boat from the USS *Kearsarge* rescues survivors from the sinking CSS *Alabama*. *Library of Congress*

along with about 40 others of the *Alabama*'s complement, had the good fortune to be rescued from the water by a British yacht, the *Deerhound,* which
took them to England rather than turn them over to the *Kearsarge.* Seventy
more were picked up by the *Kearsarge,* and another 15 by excursion boats.

Semmes was lionized in England—British admirers replaced the sword
that he had cast into the English Channel—but he was bitter over the loss of
his ship, blaming the debacle on his defective powder and the *Kearsarge*'s
protective chains. In point of fact, the battle off Cherbourg was the Civil War
in microcosm, the gallant but outgunned South, ignoring its own shortcomings, heedlessly taking on a superior force.

During her 22 months at sea, the *Alabama* had burned 54 Federal merchant ships and had bonded 10 others. After the war, when British and U.S.
negotiators determined that Britain owed the United States a total of $15.5
million for damage caused by ships sold to the Confederacy, the amount
charged to the *Alabama*—$6.75 million—was much the highest. In addition to
her remarkable toll in merchant shipping, the *Alabama* had sunk an enemy
gunboat, the luckless *Hatteras,* and had brought untold embarrassment to the
Federal navy. Semmes's record with the *Alabama* would not be approached
by any raider until the advent of the submarine.

Yet the raider's influence on the outcome of the Civil War was almost
imperceptible. Its toll, however remarkable, represented only about 5 per-
cent of U.S. shipping; the bulk of the U.S. merchant fleet stayed in port,
transferred to neutral flags, or took their chances on the high seas. After all,
the Confederacy's three or four commerce raiders could not be everywhere.
Soaring rates for marine insurance added to the North's cost of waging war,
but such economic damage was insignificant alongside the cost of the
ground fighting in terms of either lives or material. The Northern states—
economically self-sufficient—could ignore the depredations of Confederate
raiders.

After the war Semmes suggested that the North at first could not comprehend the threat posed by Confederate commerce destroyers. Yet when the
threat materialized, he noted ruefully, the North was "too deeply engaged in
the contest to heed it."

By the summer of 1864 there was no possibility of a replacement for the
Alabama, and Semmes could have lived out the war comfortably in England.
Instead, he made his way back to the Confederacy by way of Cuba and
Mexico. In Richmond he was promoted to admiral and given command of
the James River squadron in Virginia. Following the evacuation of Richmond, he burned his boats and formed his men into a naval brigade that
served under Gen. Joseph E. Johnston in the final weeks of the war.* After

---

*Semmes's service on land toward the end of the war is considered in Chapter 19.

the war Semmes was briefly under arrest, but he was never brought to trial and supported himself with a small law practice until his death in 1877.

Raphael Semmes was not the first commerce raider in the history of naval warfare, but he was the first to operate in the age of steam and he may have been the best of all time. Notwithstanding the unavailability of any home port, he managed to keep a wooden ship at sea for nearly two years without an overhaul and without losing either a crewman or a prisoner to disease. As a strategist, he demonstrated that a nation with a weak navy could nevertheless inflict great damage on any foe with a substantial merchant fleet. It is hardly surprising that Kaiser Wilhelm II made Semmes's postwar memoirs required reading for his admirals. In both world wars, German submarine and surface raiders would refine the qualities of speed, surprise, and endurance demonstrated by the *Alabama*, but with little of Semmes's regard for the lives of prisoners and crew.

In taking on the *Kearsarge*, however, Semmes had let his emotions control his judgment. His gun crews were insufficiently trained, he underestimated the enemy, and he committed a cardinal sin: He didn't keep his powder dry.

CHAPTER 13

The Strange Fate of the CSS *Florida*

AT TIMES, it was hard to tell which side feared the CSS *Florida* more—the Federals, for whom she was one of the most destructive of the Confederate commerce destroyers, or her own officers and men, to whom she was a cranky, unreliable vessel, and, for a time, a pestilential floating coffin.

Like the *Alabama*, the only Confederate cruiser to exceed her in the destruction of Federal merchantmen, the *Florida* had been constructed in Britain under the watchful eye of the able Confederate purchasing agent, James D. Bulloch. She was the first cruiser to be constructed abroad for the Confederacy, and Bulloch took great care to avoid any action that might allow Crown authorities to seize her as a warship destined for one of the American belligerents. Questioners were told that she was the *Oreto*, under construction for the Italian navy.

Nevertheless, Federal diplomats had their suspicions. Thomas Dudley, the U.S. consul in Liverpool, reported to Secretary of State Seward in January 1862,

> The [*Oreto*], a screw gunboat, is fitting out in one of the docks at this place. She is built of iron [*sic*] and is 700 tons. She is reported for the Italian Government, but . . . circumstances connected with [the sale make] me suspicious, and cause me to believe she is intended for the South.[1]

The *Oreto* hastily departed from Liverpool on March 22, 1862, ostensibly to pick up a cargo in Palermo, Italy. In fact she steered for the Bahamas, where, after a period in which she was again the target of a British investigation, she acquired her armament and her first skipper, the 33-year-old John N. Maffitt. It would be under his command that the *Florida* would achieve her greatest renown.

Fame would be slow in coming, however, for once his batteries were in place, Maffitt began a run of bad luck. First, he discovered that through

86

some oversight his ship had no gunsights, rammers, or sponges, so that his guns were useless. This would be the first of numerous misfortunes to befall the *Florida*, but not the most serious. More ominous was an outbreak of yellow fever among the crew.

Maffitt sailed to Cuba in search of his missing ordnance stores and in hope of finding medical assistance for his stricken sailors. Soon, however, Maffitt himself was among those struck down by the "yellow jack." Unable to recruit additional crewmen and no longer welcome in Cuba, Maffitt resolved on a bold stroke—to run the Federal blockade into Mobile, Alabama, and to refit there. Flying British colors, the undermanned *Florida* made her way through the blockade in broad daylight. By the time the Federals realized that she was the *Florida*, Maffitt's twin-funneled cruiser was safely under the protecting guns of Fort Morgan.

In Mobile, Maffitt recruited a new crew and awaited an opportunity to return to the high seas. He spent four months in Mobile, causing Secretary of the Navy Mallory, in Richmond, to wonder whether he intended to go to sea at all. Mallory need not have worried. On the evening of January 15, 1863, a violent storm struck the Alabama coast, and it was all that the Federal blockaders could do to keep station. At 2:00 A.M. on the 16th, Maffitt weighed anchor and made for the bar at full speed. Three Federal warships were offshore, but only one spotted the *Florida* in the driving rain, and the Rebel cruiser escaped into the gray winter mist.

The *Florida's* greatest single asset may have been her first commander, John Newland Maffitt. Born at sea in 1819 to a mother en route to the New World from Ireland, Maffitt would later list his birthplace as Longtitude 40 W, Latitude 50 N.[2] He was brought up in North Carolina and awarded a midshipman's warrant at the tender age of 13. Over the two decades, Maffitt served on a variety of ships in the U.S. Navy. He became a thorough master of his profession, with a special interest in hydrography. Tall and barrel-chested, Maffitt had a full head of curly hair. He wore his cap at a jaunty angle, his broad features tapering into a less-than-full beard. His Confederate navy colleague, Raphael Semmes, commander of the *Alabama*, wrote of Maffitt, "He knew everybody, and everybody knew him. . . . Being a jaunty, handsome fellow, he was a great favorite with the ladies."[3]

Under the bold Maffitt, the *Florida* now began the most destructive phase of her career. International law, as interpreted during the Civil War, made enemy property at sea subject to capture and confiscation. This situation meant that any maritime power was vulnerable, because not even the most powerful country could protect its entire merchant fleet from an enemy with seagoing warships. Technology, moreover, was a boon to commerce raiding. With a fresh breeze from their best quarter, many sailing vessels of the 1860s could hold their own against a steamer like the *Florida*. But the *Florida's*

CSS *Florida* by an unknown artist. *U.S. Navy Imaging Center*

ability to make 10 or 11 knots all day, without regard to wind, made her a deadly predator at a time when virtually all merchantmen were sailing ships.

Although designed as a commerce raider, the *Florida* had armament equal to that of many of the Federal vessels that would pursue her. She carried 7-inch Blakely rifles as pivot guns fore and aft, and mounted six 32-pounders in broadside.

After escaping from Mobile, Maffitt touched briefly at Cuba for fuel, for the *Florida* consumed coal in prodigious quantities. He then was off on a cruise that would see him capture 24 Federal merchantmen during the first eight months of 1863.

Had this been the War of 1812, such a string of captures would have made the officers and crew of the *Florida* wealthy. Maffitt would have manned the captured vessels with a prize crew, and sent them to the nearest Southern port. There the ships and cargo would have been sold, and the proceeds divided between the Confederate government and the complement of the *Florida*. This was 1863, however, and the Federal blockade made it almost impossible for any Confederate raider to send her prize to a friendly port.

As a result, Maffitt would burn all but five of the ships he captured. The remaining five, whose masters had papers identifying their cargoes as neutral, were released under ransom bonds, which obligated their owners to pay a specified sum to the Confederate government after the war. Ultimately, of course, such bonds would never be redeemed.

Off Cuba, Maffitt burned three Federal brigs, the *Estelle*, the *Windward*, and the *Corris Ann*. Moving northward he captured a China clipper, the *Jacob Bell*, after a six-hour chase. The *Jacob Bell*, returning to New York from Foochow, had a rich cargo, including tea, camphor, and spices. Evaluated by the Confederates at $1.5 million, the *Jacob Bell* was the most valuable ship and cargo captured by any Confederate vessel during the war. Maffitt ordered her burned.[4]

At the end of March 1863 Maffitt left the Caribbean for the Atlantic off Brazil. There, in the sea-lanes traversed by ships headed for South America and the Pacific, the *Florida* and the *Alabama* between them destroyed 25 Federal vessels during a three-month period. The one U.S. cruiser stationed off Brazil, the *Mohican*, never caught up with either Confederate raider and would have found its hands full if she had.

The U.S. shipping industry was on its way to being ruined by the Confederacy's tiny navy. During 1863, 348 U.S. ships, totaling 252,579 tons, would be sold to British interests—four times the tonnage transferred the previous year.[5] In the North, meetings were held and resolutions passed denouncing Semmes and Maffitt and imploring the Navy Department to do something about the Rebel cruisers. Secretary of the Navy Welles, reluctant to take any action that might weaken the blockade, did little more than to order a warship to the scene of the most recent burning. London's *Punch* ran a limerick,

> There was an old fogy named Welles,
> Quite worthy of cap and bells,
> For he thot that a pirate,
> Who steamed at a great rate,
> Would wait to be riddled with shells.[6]

The *Florida* left Brazilian waters in early June, working her way north. There was no shortage of enemy shipping, but Maffitt was having difficulty with his ship's engines, and called at Bermuda for coal and repairs. He stayed 11 days, long enough to enjoy the hospitality invariably accorded Confederate warships in the ports of the British Empire. On July 24, however, the *Florida*'s idyll came to a sudden end when the USS *Wachusett*, a 1,032-ton screw sloop mounting 10 guns, appeared in St. George's harbor. But the governor reminded her commander, Charles Fleming, that under international law the *Florida* was entitled to a 24-hour head start before the U.S. cruiser could pursue her. Fleming watched helplessly on July 27 as Maffitt weighed anchor and steamed out of the harbor on a course for Europe.[7]

The *Florida* made three captures en route to Europe, but her engineers were having increasing difficulty with her machinery. Convinced that his ship required a major overhaul, Maffitt chose to go to a French harbor, Brest.

Nor was Maffitt himself in good shape; after reaching Brest on August 18, he asked to be relieved because of ill health. Since he had almost died from yellow fever the previous year, the request was a reasonable one. While the *Florida* underwent her refit at a commercial shipyard, Maffit was replaced as her skipper by Comdr. Charles M. Morris.

The *Florida* remained in Brest for more than five months. Considering this time, it is nothing short of scandalous that the Federals failed to ensure that she would never again take to the high seas. With the U.S. Navy now approaching 600 vessels, Welles could have posted a squadron at all important sea-lanes, including the approaches to Brest, without significantly weakening the blockade. Instead, only one U.S. warship—the USS *Kearsarge*, commanded by John Winslow— was assigned to watch the *Florida*. There were three channels out of Brest, and Winslow would be hard-pressed to intercept the raider. Interestingly, in the light of the *Florida*'s ultimate fate, Winslow appears to have been prepared to ignore the 24-hour rule in dealing with the raider. He advised Welles on September 18, "I shall provision, and before she is ready to leave take my station outside to intercept her."[8]

The next month a second Confederate cruiser, the *Georgia*, entered the channel port of Cherbourg. Now obliged to cover two ports 170 miles apart, Winslow begged the Navy Department for reinforcements. None came. By late January the *Kearsarge* itself was so badly in need of repairs that Winslow made for Cadiz, Spain. When he returned on February 19, the *Florida* was gone. Winslow would have to wait for his moment of glory, which would come the following year against Raphael Semmes and the *Alabama*.

Charles M. Morris, Maffitt's successor as skipper of the *Florida*, was part of a pool of Confederate navy officers living in London and Paris. The Confederacy had far more professional naval officers than it had ships, and Morris considered himself fortunate to have been chosen to command the *Florida*. A native of Georgia, he had briefly commanded a Confederate gunboat out of Savannah, the *Huntress*. Subsequently, he had been chosen to command one of the rams under construction in Britain for the Confederacy; when Britain blocked the sale of these vessels, however, Morris had no command.

So it was that Morris took the *Florida* back to sea when Winslow was otherwise occupied. Notwithstanding her extended refit in Brest, the *Florida* continued to be plagued with mechanical problems, difficulties that were exacerbated by a shortage of qualified engineers. Gradually, however, Morris worked his way west, and by late June the *Florida* was active in the sea lanes off the U.S. East Coast. On July 10, near Baltimore, Morris made four captures on a single day, burning three of his prizes and bonding the fourth. Anticipating correctly that the Federals would now concentrate ships off the Maryland coast, Morris made for the Canary Islands and then for Brazil.

Despite his mechanical problems, he had added 13 more prizes to the *Florida*'s 24 captures under Maffitt. On October 4 the *Florida* entered the Brazilian port of Bahia (now Salvador).

When the *Florida* dropped anchor in Bahia's harbor on that October evening, her officers could make out the silhouette of a warship on the far side of the harbor. The morning light revealed her to be the USS *Wachusett*, Napoleon Collins, commanding. The 50-year-old Collins was a Pennsylvania-born officer of the U.S. Navy. He had seen some action during the Mexican War, but his service in the Civil War had been undistinguished and at times controversial. While commanding the 830-ton side-wheeler *Octarara*, he had seized a British vessel, the *Mont Blanc*, off an uninhabited island in the Bahamas. The British had protested that this action had taken place in British territorial waters, and the Lincoln administration had returned the ship with an apology. Within the U.S. Navy, however, there was considerable sympathy for Collins, and there is no evidence that he was chastened by the pro forma reprimand he had received.[9]

Brazilian authorities knew little of Collins's past, but with enemy warships in their harbor the Brazilians took action designed to preclude any impulsive move by either commander. A Brazilian corvette, the *Dona Januaria*, anchored between the two belligerent, and local authorities exacted a promise from both commanders that they would not initiate hostilities in the harbor. At Morris's request, the *Florida* was allowed 48 hours in which to coal.

As he reflected on his position, Collins felt increasingly frustrated. Because the *Florida* was entitled to a 24-hour head start once she weighed anchor, it was highly unlikely that *Wachusett* could capture her at sea. What was he to do? He first sent Morris a challenge through the U.S. consul, Thomas F. Wilson, inviting the Confederate to bring his ship outside the three-mile limit and to fight the *Wachusett* there. John Maffitt might have jumped at such an opportunity for battle, but Charles Morris was all too aware of his ship's shortcomings, and his orders were to avoid combat with enemy cruisers. Morris told an intermediary that he would "neither seek nor avoid" combat with the *Wachusett*, a statement that was tantamount to declining Collins's challenge.

Under most circumstances, Federal diplomats in a port like Bahia might have insisted on strict adherence to international law by visiting ships of the U.S. Navy. This was not the case, however, with Consul Wilson at Bahia. Because the 24-hour rule made it likely that the *Florida* would eventually elude the *Wachusett*, Wilson urged Collins to seize or destroy the raider in port. Collins did not immediately agree to such an egregious violation of Brazilian waters, but agreed to consult with his officers. When all except one of them supported Wilson, Collins was won over. He agreed to attack the raider and began to make the necessary preparations. To ensure secrecy, no crew members were allowed ashore.[10]

Unaware of what was taking place on the *Wachusett*, Morris had been granting liberty to his crewmen, one watch at a time. When the port watch returned on the evening of October 6, Morris and several other officers joined the starboard watch on shore. While his sailors sought out bars and bordellos, Morris attended a ballet in the town theater. Meanwhile, Collins moved ahead with his plans, raising steam and sending a whaleboat to reconnoiter the *Florida*. His intention was to ram his enemy, to sink her without firing a shot, and then head to sea. When *Wachusett*'s boat returned, he heard his officer's report but kept the boat in the water, lest the sound of its being hoisted alert the *Florida*'s watch.

At 3:00 A.M. on October 7, when the harbor was almost still, the *Wachusett* slipped her cables. Circling to avoid the *Dona Januaria*, Collins bore down on the *Florida*. His plan, however, quickly went awry. The *Wachusett* was not able to build up much speed in the confines of the harbor. Moreover, instead of ramming the *Florida* amidships, Collins struck his target a glancing blow on her starboard quarter, carrying away the mizzen mast and some bulwarks but not doing enough damage to sink her. Collins was backing away when the skeleton crew aboard the *Florida* began firing small arms. The crew of the *Wachusett* replied. Contrary to Collins's orders, his executive officer, Lester Beardslee, employed his 32-pounders as well as small arms.

In response to Collins's demand for surrender, Lt. Thomas Porter, the senior officer left on the *Florida*, boarded the *Wachusett* and surrendered, even as he protested the attack in neutral waters. Collins ordered a line attached to the *Florida* and towed her out to sea. When the Brazilians awoke to what was happening, there were shots from the fort overlooking the harbor, and three Brazilian gunships set out in pursuit. Even with the *Florida* in tow, however, *Wachusett* outdistanced her pursuers.[11]

The *Florida* was done as a commerce raider, but her story was by no means over. Had Collins sunk the raider at her anchorage, he would have had a bit of explaining to do but he would have accomplished his objective. Indeed, had he arranged for his prize to sink off Bahia, he would have been welcomed in Washington. But in bringing the *Florida*, seized in such dubious circumstances, to American waters, Collins was asking for trouble. He may have reached this conclusion himself, for his behavior on the voyage to Hampton Roads, Virginia, was notably erratic. First he had trouble with Lieutenant Beardslee, whom he had put in command of the *Florida*. According to charges that he would make later, Beardslee failed to keep within sight of the *Wachusett*, prompting the irate Collins to threaten to fire upon his prize. Beardslee, in turn, in a written message to Collins, warned that should the

Wachusett at any time begin firing at the *Florida*, "I should . . . be led to the belief that the Confederates aboard the *Wachusett* had captured the vessel and that my duty to my country called upon me to destroy her."[12]

Meanwhile, on shore, Charles Morris had been awakened by the proprietor of his hotel with word that there was some trouble on board his ship. Once he had learned the fate of the *Florida*, he filed a protest with Brazilian authorities against the Federals' "barbarous and piratical act." There was a certain irony in Morris's protest; since the beginning of the war, the Federals had attempted to paint the Confederate cruisers as nothing more than pirates. Now the tables were turned.

Meanwhile, Collins's behavior was becoming increasingly paranoid. Faced with a long voyage home and fearful that the 70-odd prisoners from the *Florida* might attempt to take over the *Wachusett*, Collins first kept them in irons. Then, during layovers at St. Bartholomew and later at St. Thomas, he permitted prisoners to escape. After leaving St. Thomas, the *Wachusett* and her prize arrived at Hampton Roads on November 12. The two vessels had taken more than a month to make the 4,500-mile voyage from Bahia to Hampton Roads. There, Adm. David D. Porter ordered the *Florida* anchored at the exact spot where the Confederate *Merrimack* had rammed and sunk the USS *Cumberland* more than two years earlier.

Satisfaction in Washington over the seizure of the *Florida* was tempered by recognition that the administration had a diplomatic problem on its hands. The Brazilian government had protested Collins's violation of its territorial waters and demanded that the United States disavow his action. Then "fate" intervened in the form of an army transport, the *Alliance*. On November 19 the *Florida* was damaged in an unexplained collision with the *Alliance*. The raider's pumps had been able to handle the leaks from her ramming by the *Wachusett*, but after the curious affair with the *Alliance* it proved difficult to keep the Confederate vessel afloat. On November 28, Porter telegraphed Welles that the *Florida* had sunk during the night.[13]

The disappearance of a prize such as the *Florida* required some explanation, and Porter convened a court of inquiry. Meeting in early December, the court concluded that the *Florida* had sunk as a result of the failure of the donkey engine that operated her pumps. The court faulted the fireman on watch for failing to inform the engineer of the breakdown, and noted in passing that "some of the deck pumps were out of order." However, no disciplinary action was recommended.[14]

On December 26, Secretary of State Seward formally replied to the protest from Brazil. After first insisting that no Confederate vessel was entitled to the rights accorded belligerents, Seward conceded that Collins had acted without authority, as had Consul Wilson. Collins would appear before a court-martial, and Wilson, who admitted that he had "advised and incited" Collins, would be dismissed. As for the *Florida*, "It is assumed that the loss of the *Florida* was a consequence of some unforeseen accident which cast no responsibility upon the United States."[15]

The court-martial of Napoleon Collins took place on the USS *Baltimore* on April 7, 1865. President of the court was Adm. Louis M. Goldsborough, who for much of the war had commanded the North Atlantic Blockading Squadron. In what would prove to be one of the briefest courts on record, Collins was charged with having violated the territory of Brazil in attacking the *Florida* in Bahia harbor. Collins plead guilty, adding, "I respectfully request that it may be entered on the records of the court as my defense that the capture of the *Florida* was for the public good."[16]

The sentence of the court was nevertheless draconian, for it called for Collins's dismissal from the navy. Collins returned to his home in Burlington, New Jersey, prepared to appeal but perhaps thinking that his navy career was over. In September, however, Secretary Welles set aside the court's verdict and restored Collins to active service. He eventually was promoted to rear admiral; he was commander of the South Pacific Squadron when he died in 1875.[17]

In the bars of Norfolk and Newport News, there would long be stories about how the *Florida* had come to sink at her moorings. Some of these reached John Maffitt, who was attempting to earn a livelihood in Wilmington, North Carolina, after the war. Maffitt had friends and admirers in the U.S. Navy, and on a visit to Washington, D.C., in 1872, he called on Admiral Porter. The subject turned to the *Florida*, and Maffitt asked what had really happened to his old command. Maffitt took notes on what Porter told him:

> During an interview between Mr. Seward and Admiral Porter the former exclaimed, "I wish [the *Florida*] was at the bottom of the sea!" "Do you mean it?" exclaimed Porter. "I do, from my soul," was the answer. "It shall be done," replied Porter. Admiral Porter placed an engineer in charge of the stolen steamer, his imperative instructions being, "Before midnight open the sea cock and do not leave that engine room until the water is up to your chin. At sunrise that rebel craft must be a thing of the past resting on the bottom of the sea."

> At daylight the *Florida* was no longer to be seen. . . . Eventually the principal actor [i.e., Porter] avowed the deed as instigated by the Secretary of State to avoid the reparation demanded by Brazil and urged by the diplomatic representatives of Europe.[18]

The strange fate of the *Florida* was a tribute to the Federal government's belated fear of Confederate cruisers. The Lincoln administration was determined that the redoubtable *Florida* would never take to sea again.

CHAPTER 14

Hancock the Superb

MILITARY LIVES are defined in a few vital moments. The surgeon buries his mistakes and the failed merchant starts anew. For the professional soldier, however, years of training and peacetime routine may climax in a few critical battlefield decisions—often based on incomplete information—that will determine who will live and which army emerge victorious.

Some soldiers seem to have been created for such moments. One such man was Maj. Gen. Winfield Scott Hancock, who in June 1863 commanded one of the three corps that made up the Army of the Potomac. On June 28 that luckless army had just been given its fourth commanding general in two years, George G. Meade. Three days later, Meade's army was locked in what would prove to be the decisive battle of the Civil War.

When Federal and Confederate units first met at Gettysburg on July 1, the commander of the I Corps, Gen. John F. Reynolds, was an early fatality. Meade, then at Taneytown, had called Hancock to his headquarters and ordered him to take command of all Union forces at Gettysburg. Meade did not go himself, for he was not yet convinced that the fighting there involved Lee's main force. Reaching Cemetery Hill about 3:30 P.M., Hancock studied the field and recommended to Meade that the army fight there.

Two days later, as Lee readied his last, desperate assault, the Confederates opened one of the heaviest artillery barrages of the war. In an act of both bravery and bravado, Hancock chose this time to inspect his lines, mounted on a black sorrel, his staff behind him. Hancock's intent, according to one officer, was to show every soldier that "his general was behind him in the storm."[1] Hancock was not behind his men, he was in front of them, and his famous ride made him one of the heroes of Gettysburg. Remarkably, he completed his inspection without injury, only to incur a painful wound during Pickett's charge.

Winfield Scott Hancock was born in 1824, one of twin boys whose father was a Norristown, Pennsylvania, attorney. His father named him for the country's most famous living soldier, and young Winfield demonstrated an early interest in schoolyard war games. But as a young man he became interested in the law as well, and not even his career in the army ended his interest in his father's profession. Benjamin Hancock instilled in his son a strict constructionist's reverence for the Constitution, and when young Hancock set off for West Point in the fall of 1840 he took with him a copy of Blackstone's *Commentaries*.

Hancock's record at the military academy was not outstanding; he was best remembered for his talent in drawing. But he graduated in time to see service in Mexico, where he was breveted first lieutenant for "gallant and meritorious conduct" in the battles at Contreras and Churubusco. Hancock remained in Mexico City after its capture by his namesake, Winfield Scott. The effectiveness of Scott's benign military rule was not lost on Hancock who, two decades later, would administer part of the conquered Confederacy.

On his return to the United States, Hancock had two brief frontier postings before being ordered to Jefferson Barracks outside St. Louis. There he courted and married Almira Russell, the daughter of a prominent local merchant. A succession of frontier postings followed, and although the young officer may have been tempted to throw over the army for the law, he persevered. In 1857, while in Kansas, he was attached to the expedition headed by Col. Albert Sidney Johnston to establish Federal sovereignty over Mormon settlements in Utah. From Utah he was posted to Los Angeles, to serve as quartermaster for army garrisons on the West Coast.

When news of Fort Sumter reached Los Angeles, Hancock immediately requested orders to Washington. But the mills ground slowly, and the Hancocks found themselves exchanging farewells with Southern colleagues who had thrown in their lot with the Confederacy. One such friend was Lewis Armistead, whose friendship with Hancock, unshaken by war, would be a subplot in the 1993 movie *Gettysburg*. Hancock was a good listener, and his later record suggests that he had little sympathy for abolitionist agitation in the North. But he had even less interest in the secessionist arguments of his Southern comrades, remarking to his wife on one occasion that he did not belong to a country "formed of principalities."[2]

Not until August 1861 did Hancock receive orders to report to Washington. His timing, however, was good. The new commander of the Army of the Potomac, George B. McClellan, was looking for West Pointers as he trained a force with which to avenge the debacle at First Manassas. Hancock, who had aspired to command a regiment, found himself commanding a brigade as McClellan launched his ambitious campaign against Richmond by way of the James Peninsula. Hancock's first important action was at

Gen. Winfield S. Hancock, said to be one of the handsomest soldiers in the U.S. Army. *Library of Congress*

Williamsburg, where on May 5, 1862, he repulsed an attack by a superior Confederate force. It was little more than a skirmish, but McClellan's report to Washington included the line "Hancock was superb!" The North had need of heroes, and from that time forth he was the "Superb" Hancock.

In the midst of the Battle of Antietam, one of McClellan's division commanders, Israel B. Richardson, was fatally wounded. McClellan sent for Hancock and ordered him to take command of Richardson's division, which occupied a key position in the Federal center. Hancock did not especially distinguish himself in that bloody stalemate, but his elevation to division command brought promotion to major general and began an association with the II Corps that would continue for most of the war.

Hancock was a "McClellan man." His admiration for the army commander was as genuine as that of any soldier in the ranks. He marveled at McClellan's organizational gifts and was too busy with his own responsibilities to reflect on "Little Mac's" lack of strategic aggressiveness and his failure, as at Antietam, to bring the full force of his army against the enemy. When Lincoln supplanted McClellan with Burnside in November 1862,

Hancock wrote his wife that "the Army are not satisfied with the change, and consider the treatment of McClellan most ungracious and inopportune."[3]

Hancock participated in the abortive Federal attack on Fredericksburg, a debacle that doubtless strengthened his regard for the departed McClellan. He was in the thick of battle at Chancellorsville where he had two horses shot from under him while covering the Federal retreat. No matter what the fate of the Army of the Potomac, Hancock's personal star continued to rise. He combined a charismatic presence on the battlefield with the professional soldier's respect for matters of maneuver and logistics. There were even a few who thought that Hancock should command the army. He wrote to his wife after Chancellorsville, "I have been approached again in connection with the command of the Army of the Potomac. Give yourself no uneasiness—under no conditions would I accept the command. I do not belong to that class of generals who the Republicans care to build up."[4]

The commander of the II Corps, Gen. Darius Couch—contemptuous of Hooker's leadership—asked to be relieved after Chancellorsville. On June 9, President Lincoln acceded to Couch's request and made Hancock his successor. Less than three weeks later, while the Army of the Potomac shadowed Lee's second invasion of the North, the president replaced Hooker with Meade. Two great armies were edging northward when foragers from Lee's army precipitated the great clash at Gettysburg.

Hancock's Gettysburg wound was serious, and it almost disabled him for the remainder of the war. A bullet had passed through his saddle, driving a nail and small pieces of wood into his abdomen. Given the state of medicine in those times it is remarkable that he survived; as it was, he had a long convalescence at Norristown, during which he again became the subject of speculation as a commander of the Army of the Potomac. But when Grant assumed overall command of the Federal armies and launched his offensive against Lee in May 1864, Hancock was back with the II Corps, traveling much of the time in an ambulance. Regis de Trobriand, a Frenchman serving with the Federal forces, left this portrait of the general:

> General Hancock is one of the handsomest men in the United States Army. He is tall in stature, robust in figure, with movements of easy dignity. . . . His manners are generally very polite. His voice is pleasant, and his speech as agreeable as his looks. Such is Hancock in repose.

> In action he is entirely different. Dignity gives way to activity; his features become animated, his voice loud, his eyes are on fire . . . and his bearing is that of a man carried away by passion—the character of bravery. It is this, I think, which renders him much less fit for an independent command than to act under orders.[5]

Hancock was prominent in much of the fall campaign. The II Corps's surprise assault on the "mule shoe" salient at Spottsylvania provided the Federals with one of the more conspicuous successes of a costly and exhausting campaign. In the Army of the Potomac, as elsewhere, the forthcoming presidential election came to be seen as a referendum on the war. Notwithstanding his friendship for the Democratic candidate, McClellan, Hancock cast a vote for Lincoln. By this time his wound was causing such discomfort that Grant decided that Hancock should not winter at the front. Instead, he was sent north to recruit a "veterans corps" that he would command the following spring.

The veterans corps was not a success. Not even Hancock could compete against the bonuses being offered to soldiers to enlist in existing units. On February 27, 1865, he was given command of the Middle Department, an area that included northern Virginia and the nation's capital. Following Lee's surrender, Hancock negotiated for several days with the most prominent of the Confederate partisan commanders, John S. Mosby, before Mosby agreed to the same terms as had been granted Lee. Mosby's surgeon quoted Hancock as expressing sympathy for the Confederates "in what you believe to be a great misfortune. You have fought bravely and have nothing to be ashamed of."[6]

Because Washington, D.C., was in his military district, Hancock found himself involved in the execution of John Wilkes Booth's accomplices, including Mary Surratt. There was considerable overlap in military jurisdictions at that time, but when Hancock became a possible candidate for the presidency, opponents within his own party would accuse him of having been cruel and unfeeling in his dealings with Mrs. Surratt. Actually, Hancock appears to have been appalled at the prospect of hanging any woman, and to have taken small steps to ease the conditions of her confinement.

The following year saw Hancock—by then a major general in the regular army—in command of the Department of the Missouri, with headquarters at Fort Leavenworth. He might have served the remainder of his career as a political neutral had not President Johnson sought him out for a controversial appointment. Midway through his term, Johnson chose Hancock to command one of the military districts into which the former Confederacy had been divided under the first of the Reconstruction Acts. Johnson had opposed the legislation, but many Northerners were upset about the ease with which the states of the former Confederacy were returning erstwhile secessionists to positions of power, while keeping the freedmen politically powerless.

Of all the military districts, none was more volatile than the Fifth, comprising Louisiana and Texas. New Orleans had been the scene of repeated black demonstrations, which had led to bloody riots. Emissaries sent to the scene by Johnson had emphasized the disruptive role played by carpetbag orators, and had portrayed the district commander, Gen. Phil Sheridan, as their protector. Johnson, sympathetic to the viewpoint of Southern whites, looked for a successor to Sheridan with a more conciliatory approach. His choice fell on Hancock, and acceptance of the post brought the Pennsylvania soldier into the political arena with a vengeance.

Hancock reported to New Orleans in the autumn of 1867 against the advice of General Grant, who had urged him not to associate himself with Johnson's policies. On November 29, Hancock issued his first order as district commander, one that made clear that his would be a loose rein. Even under military rule, he announced, rights such as trial by jury, habeas corpus, and liberty of the press were paramount. Crime "must be left to the consideration and judgment of the regular civil tribunals, and these tribunals will be supported in their lawful jurisdiction."[7]

General Order No. 40, as it was titled, made Hancock a hero in the South. It held out the promise that, notwithstanding military defeat, there was hope for the old social order. Hancock understood the furor his order would set off, but the order reflected his understanding that civil law was paramount in peacetime. He may also have suspected that a prominent soldier who took such a stand would have a future in politics.

Unfortunately for Hancock, his chief supporter in Washington, Johnson, had been largely neutralized by the growing strength of the Radical Republicans. Grant himself was moving closer to the Radicals, and in February 1868, after Hancock had removed members of the New Orleans city council for overstepping their authority, Grant ordered them returned to office. Hancock protested the order at length, giving reasons for his action and asking for a hearing. Grant refused, adding with regard to Hancock's long telegram that "despatches of such length . . . should be sent by mail."[8]

Johnson sent a special message to Congress praising Hancock's administration in Texas and Louisiana. The president himself was about to be impeached, however, and Hancock about to be removed. On March 14, as Johnson defended himself before the Senate, Grant ordered Hancock to report to Washington. This latter-day "Battle of New Orleans" made Hancock many friends in the South, but created a rift between him and Grant that ended only when Hancock called on the dying Grant nearly two decades later. The immediate effect was to make Hancock a hot political property. Without even expressing interest in the nomination, he almost became the Democratic presidential nominee against Grant in 1868. Hancock at one time led in the voting at the Democratic convention; ultimately, however, the nomination went to a longtime politico, Horatio Seymour of New York.

In the years that followed Hancock was not often in the public eye, and when he was the situation was not one to improve his political prospects. For several years he was exiled to the West, where he attempted to deal with the intractable conflicts between the Indians and white settlers. While he was

largely indifferent to the fate of the freedmen, he respected the treaty rights
of the Indian tribes. As commander of the Department of Dakota in 1872, he
attempted to halt the influx of gold prospectors into the Black Hills. He
noted in a proclamation that the government had pledged to protect the
Black Hills from white encroachment. He would, accordingly, use troops if
necessary to prevent prospectors from infiltrating the area.[9]

In 1877 Hancock returned to the East, where it fell to him to put down
riots growing out of a strike by railroad workers. Hancock appears to have
had no compunction about using army forces to maintain order; all he required was that the army observe the proper legal forms. His attitude reflects
a willingness to undertake unpopular assignments, but it also suggests—as
did his General Order No. 40—an unwillingness to look beyond the legality
of a given course of action.

In the postwar years Hancock maintained a friendly correspondence with
Gen. William T. Sherman, who occasionally intervened with Grant on
Hancock's behalf. Sherman once needled his friend about the problems that
Hancock's political leanings caused him, prompting Hancock to reply,

> I can assure you that my purposes and intentions have been and
> still are to serve the Government of the United States faithfully
> and to the best of my ability. . . . Referring to my public career, I
> retract nothing which I have said and apologize for nothing I have
> done. . . .
>
> If the danger you apprehend materialized alike for all officers who
> take any part whatever in political affairs, I could understand it.
> But I judge from your letter that only those who have opposed the
> party in power are in peril, while those—some in high rank, who
> have taken an open and active part in *support* of that party—are to
> pass without penalty.[10]

All things considered, the Hancock of the late 1870s no longer suggested
a hot political property. Physically, he had entered a portly middle age, and
he had been largely out of the public eye. Nevertheless, some leaders of the
Democratic Party believed that the best way to lay to rest the "party of
treason" label which they had worn since the Civil War would be to nomi-
nate a candidate with impeccable war credentials. Many party leaders favored the renomination of Samuel J. Tilden, who had been deprived of the
presidency by some blatant political chicanery in the disputed election of
1876. But when Tilden took himself out of the running shortly before the
1880 convention, the field was wide open. Hancock was nominated on the
second ballot. As his running mate against the Republican ticket of Garfield and Arthur the Democrats chose a wealthy Indiana businessman, William H. English.

The Democrats faced an uphill fight. The Hayes administration had gone far in retrieving the GOP from the mire in which it had been left by President Grant. Times were good. In Garfield the Republicans had a leader who was a popular member of Congress and a skilled conciliator of differences within his party. Finally, the Republicans had a strong grass-roots organization, based in part on war veterans—the Grand Army of the Republic.

The campaign of 1880 saw the flowering of the "front porch" campaign. Garfield's front porch was in Mentor, Ohio; Hancock's was at Governor's Island, New York. Although Hancock maintained a heavy correspondence with leaders of his party and other supporters, his attitude toward the campaign was somewhat remote. His letter accepting the nomination made it clear that his was a mission of national reconciliation.

As the campaign went on, the Republicans introduced an issue of which Hancock did not approve. The Democrats had earlier endorsed a tariff "for revenue only"—language the Republicans interpreted as abandoning any tariff protection for American industry. For the first time since Jackson's day the tariff emerged as an important issue, and the Democrats found themselves on the defensive. Hancock was roundly criticized for his naïveté when, in an interview, he characterized the tariff as a local rather than a national issue. Cartoonist Thomas Nast, a loyal Republican, portrayed the Democratic candidate—about to deliver a speech—asking a colleague, "Who is Tariff, and why is he for revenue only?"[11]

Nor was this the end of Hancock's woes. Sensing a trend toward the Republicans, the Democrats committed a blunder that may have proved decisive. On October 20 an obscure New York City tabloid published what purported to be a letter from Garfield to one H. L. Morey of Lynn, Massachusetts. In the letter, Garfield declared that Chinese immigration should not be halted "until our great manufacturing and corporate interests are conserved." Companies had a right "to buy labor where they can get it cheapest."[12]

The "Morey letter" caused an immediate sensation. Garfield branded it as false, and his claim was substantiated when handwriting experts confirmed that the letter was a clumsy forgery. Moreover, the Republicans were able to demonstrate to most people's satisfaction that there was no such person as H. L. Morey in Lynn, Massachusetts.

So Hancock's campaign ended on a distinctly muted note. When the ballots were counted on November 2, Garfield was shown to have won 215 electoral votes to 155 for Hancock and the Democrats. The election had in fact turned on New York, where disunity among the Democrats cost Hancock 35 votes and the election. In terms of the popular vote, the election of 1880 was one of the closest ever; Garfield's popular plurality was some 10,000 out of more than 9 million votes cast. Paradoxically, the erstwhile Union hero of Gettysburg carried every state of the former Confederacy.

The general did not stay up for late returns. In his wife's words,

> At 7 o'clock P.M. on the day of the election, he yielded to the extreme weariness and prostration which ensued from his five months' labors and went to bed, begging me under no circumstances to disturb him. . . . At 5 o'clock on the following morning he inquired of me the news. I replied, "It has been a complete Waterloo for you." "That is all right," he said, "I can stand it," and in another moment he was again asleep.[13]

After his unsuccessful election campaign Hancock returned to his army duties, which he had never truly laid down. Two years earlier he had helped to found the Military Service Institution of the United States, and now he became its first president. Not since Jefferson's day had there been a professional society for army and navy officers, and the Civil War had brought a quickening of interest in the profession of arms.

Although Hancock's own political career was ended, his interest in politics was undiminished. Four years after his defeat for the presidency he wrote to an old supporter, Sen. James Doolittle of Wisconsin, about the campaign:

> I understood the Democratic campaign of 1880 to have for its purpose: the restoration of privity of elections, the return to simplicity and economy in the public business, the reestablishment of harmony, mutual confidence and prosperity throughout the different parts of the country, the purification of the fountains of justice, & generally, the impartial, faithful and efficient administration of the government.

With regard to the tariff, he had not called it a "local issue," but the term was appropriate:

> It is a question, as I said at the time, which affects localities differently; and as the people in the various Congressional districts elect Members of Congress to represent their interests, the original presentation and discussion of [tariffs] should occur among the people of the various localities when choosing their Representatives.[14]

Two years later, in 1886, Hancock died after a short illness. Tributes came from political leaders like President Cleveland and Governor Tilden, and from soldiers like Phil Sheridan and Joseph E. Johnston. The obituaries emphasized his military career, for the country was still reliving the Civil War. But some observers remembered his role in reconciling the South. Secretary of State Thomas Bayard paid tribute to a soldier who, "like Washington, never forgot he was also a citizen."[15]

Politically, Hancock had much in common with Grover Cleveland. Both were staunchly conservative and not notably imaginative, but each possessed an integrity that commanded respect. It seems more than coincidental that a sentence from Hancock's acceptance speech in 1880, "A public office is a trust," became the byword of Cleveland's successful campaign four years later.

In his unsuccessful campaign Hancock carried the South so convincingly as to establish the tradition of a "solid South" that stood the Democrats in good stead well into the 20th century. A Charleston, South Carolina, newspaper remarked on the warmth felt in the former Confederacy toward their one-time antagonist:

> The South has changed but little in some respects since the . . . men who recoiled from Hancock's lines at Gettysburg began the retreat which ended at Appomattox. But the men who stood with him on the summit of the hill that day, and who cheered him as he rode along the lines, scarcely mourn his loss . . . more sincerely than those whom he opposed.[16]

CHAPTER 15

The Painter and
the President

ON FEBRUARY 12, 1878, a crowd of dignitaries gathered in the rotunda of the United States Capitol for a ceremony that had been anticipated for many months. The occasion was the acceptance by the U.S. government of a famous gift—a renowned painting titled *The First Reading of the Emancipation Proclamation*, the most famous work of New York portraitist Francis B. Carpenter. The heroic painting of President Abraham Lincoln and his cabinet had been purchased from the artist by a wealthy philanthropist, Mrs. Elizabeth Thompson, for presentation to Congress.

The work was unveiled on what would have been Lincoln's 69th birthday, before a joint assembly of the Senate and House. Future president James A. Garfield, the House minority leader, and Rep. Alexander H. Stephens of Georgia, once vice president of the Confederate States of America, provided the oratory. Garfield, a frequent critic of Lincoln during the Civil War, now spoke of the late president as "one of the few great rulers whose wisdom increased with his power and whose spirit grew gentler and tenderer as his triumphs were multiplied."

When the drapery was removed and the crowd saw the painting, there was a round of applause for the artist and the famous scene he had depicted. Only a few in the audience asked themselves whether the painting looked somehow different from the way they remembered it. . . .

Francis Bicknell Carpenter was born in 1830 on a farm near the town of Homer in upstate New York. As a boy he showed an interest in art, sketching pastoral scenes on blank pages of old account books. On occasion he ob-

105

served itinerant portrait painters at work and attempted to imitate them with such materials as could be found on a farm, including vegetable dyes and the crude brushes used by carriage painters. Eventually, young Carpenter demonstrated enough talent that his father arranged for him to spend five months in Syracuse studying with a portrait artist named Sanford Thayer.

Frank Carpenter was only 16 years old when he returned from Syracuse, but he promptly set up a studio. His first commission, for $10, was to illustrate a book on sheep-raising. The author was so pleased with the result that he requested a portrait too. The favorable reception of these and other early works gave Carpenter sufficient confidence that, in 1851, he set out to ply his trade in New York City. He had been there less than a year when he married a New York girl, August Prentiss, and received a commission to paint Millard Fillmore, then president of the United States.

The Fillmore portrait, eventually bought by the city of New York, changed Carpenter's life. Suddenly, his career took off. He painted Fillmore's successor, Franklin Pierce, and in 1855 spent several months in Washington, D.C., executing portraits of political luminaries such as ex-president John Tyler and Senator William H. Seward. Most of those who sat for the genial artist—and a sitting generally required several days—came away not only satisfied customers but friends. And Carpenter, for his part, developed an interest in politics.

When the Civil War broke out in 1861, Carpenter was an outspoken supporter of the Union cause and a strong opponent of slavery. He was thrilled when, on September 22, 1862, Lincoln issued his preliminary emancipation proclamation. Carpenter was sure that it was one of the great acts of history. The proclamation announced that, with the coming of the new year, the U.S. Government would consider all slaves in the seceded states free. This meant that when slaves sought protection in the North or in the lines of the Federal armies, they would be treated as refugees, not as runaway slaves or "contraband of war." On January 1, 1863, the promises of the preliminary document were put into effect by a formal Emancipation Proclamation.

Carpenter the artist developed an overwhelming urge to depict on canvas his president's signing of the proclamation. What other single act so encapsulated the war's noble purpose? But Carpenter had no contacts in the Lincoln White House and he badly needed a sponsor. One possibility was Rep. Owen Lovejoy, an abolitionist congressman from Illinois and a friend of Lincoln. Carpenter wrote Lovejoy on January 5, 1864, explaining his intention:

> It is to paint a picture of one of the greatest subjects for a historical picture ever presented to an artist, *President Lincoln Reading the Proclamation of Independence* [sic] to his Cabinet, previous to its publication. I have been studying upon the design for the picture for

some weeks and I never felt a stronger conviction or assurance of success in any undertaking in my life! . . . I wish to paint this picture *now* while all the actors in the scene are living and while they are still in the discharge of the duties of their several high offices.

Lovejoy provided the introduction that Carpenter needed, and with assurances of financial backing from one Frederick A. Lane, the painter took a train to Washington on February 4, 1864. A White House reception on his first Saturday in the capital gave Carpenter an opportunity to meet the president.

Two o'clock found me one of the throng pressing toward the center of attraction, the "blue" room. From the threshold of the "crimson" parlor as I passed, I had a glimpse of the gaunt figure of Mr. Lincoln in the distance, haggard looking, dressed in black, relieved only by the prescribed white gloves; standing, it seemed to me, solitary and alone, though surrounded by the crowd, bending low now and then in the process of hand-shaking, and responding half abstractedly to the well-meant greetings.

Carpenter worked his way up to the president, who received a whispered word from one of his secretaries about Carpenter's project. Shaking hands, Lincoln remarked, "Oh, yes . . . this is the painter." The artist made some innocuous reply, prompting Lincoln to remark good-humoredly, "Do you think, Mr. Carpenter, that you can make a handsome picture of *me?*" Later that evening the president received Carpenter in his office. After reading his letter of introduction from Lovejoy, he turned to the artist and remarked, "Well, Mr. Carpenter, we will turn you loose here, and try to give you a good chance to work out your idea."

Carpenter moved his gear into the White House, and in mid-February began a remarkable period of six months in which he not only painted but was allowed to observe Lincoln and his often fractious associates at work. At first the painter considered setting up his canvas in the library, but lighting conditions led him to choose the State Dining Room instead. For preliminary sketches, however, he would go to the Cabinet Room, where Lincoln conducted much of his business. When one visitor, intent upon a private conversation with the president, called attention to Carpenter, Lincoln dismissed his presence with a jest, "You need not mind him; he is but a painter."

Early on, the outline of Carpenter's painting began taking shape in what the artist called "a mingling of fact and allegory." Carpenter wanted to depict Lincoln and his cabinet in relation to the great issues of war and slavery:

There were two elements in the Cabinet, the radical and the conservative. Mr. Lincoln was placed at the head of the official table, between the two groups, nearest that representing the radical, but the uniting point of both. The chief powers of government are War and Finance: the ministers of these [are] at his right.

Carpenter had arrived in Washington a supporter of the Lincoln administration. Now, as he observed the president first hand, he became an awe-struck admirer. He was fascinated by Lincoln's handling of the unending requests for pardons, some of which strained the president's well-known compassion. One woman petitioned on behalf of her son, who had been serving in the Confederate army. Hearing that his mother was ill, he had visited her in the North, only to be captured while returning to his unit. The mother now promised that her son, if released, would take the oath of allegiance to the United States and have nothing more to do with the Rebels—she gave the president her word. "Your word," repeated Lincoln, dryly. "Your son came home from fighting against his country; he was sick; you secreted him, nursed him up, and when cured, started him off again to help destroy some more of our boys." Lincoln reflected for a moment but then reached for a piece of paper and wrote on it. He handed it to her with the remark, "I just want you to understand that I have done this just to get rid of you."

During the campaign for Richmond in 1864, Carpenter asked the president how he rated Grant in comparison with other Union commanders. Lincoln replied,

> The great thing about Grant, I take it, is his perfect coolness and persistency of purpose. I judge he is not easily excited, which is a great element in an officer, and he has the grit of a bulldog! Once let him get his teeth in, and nothing can shake him off.

Carpenter came to delight in the president's penchant for story-telling. On one occasion, after a Federal military setback, the painter showed Lincoln a newspaper article that exonerated the administration from responsibility for the defeat. Lincoln responded with a story:

> A traveler on the frontier found himself [lost] one night in a most inhospitable region. A terrific thunderstorm came up, to add to his trouble. He floundered along until his horse at length gave out. The lightning afforded him the only clue to his way, but the peals of thunder were frightful. One bolt, which seemed to crash the earth beneath him, brought him to his knees. By no means a pray-ing man, his petition was short and to the point: "Oh Lord, if it is all the same to you, give us a little more light and a little less noise."

One day Gov. Andrew Curtin of Pennsylvania, together with a constitu-ent, paid the president a visit. Their business completed, Lincoln invited them into the East Room to watch Carpenter at work. Sitting on the edge of a long table, legs dangling, the president ruminated about the origins of the Emancipation Proclamation: "You see, Curtin, I was brought to the conclusion that there was no dodging this Negro question any longer. We had reached a point where it seemed that we must avail ourselves of this element, or in all probability go under."

Curtin remarked that it was believed in some quarters that Secretary of State Seward had opposed the proclamation. Lincoln replied,

> That is not true. He advised postponement at the first [cabinet] meeting, which seemed to me sound. It was Seward's persistence which resulted in the insertion of the word *maintain* [the proclamation directed Federal authorities to "recognize and maintain" the freedom of ex-slaves] which I feared under the circumstances was promising more than was quite probable we could carry out.

In creating his famous portrait Carpenter first sketched the outline on a great canvas in the State Dining Room. He became so absorbed in his work that more than once the morning light found him "still standing, pencil or palette in hand, before the immense canvas, unable to break the spell that bound me to it."

Working in an age in which photography was becoming available and affordable, Carpenter made use of this relatively new technology wherever he could. He brought one of Mathew Brady's cameramen to the White House to take pictures of some members of the cabinet and objects in the Cabinet Room, and worked from these photographs while executing his painting.

On one occasion, photographers stored their paraphernalia in a closet that Lincoln's son, Tad, regarded as his private preserve. The 10-year-old locked the closet and ignored even his father's entreaties to return the key. Eventually, Lincoln followed his son into the family quarters and returned in a few minutes with the key. According to Lincoln, he had asked Tad whether he realized he was causing his father a great deal of trouble and the boy, bursting into tears, had immediately surrendered the key.

Carpenter reveled in his access to the White House. Although he could produce a routine portrait in a few days, he managed to spin out his work on the Emancipation Proclamation for half a year. By July 1864, however, the work was complete. One afternoon, as Lincoln was preparing for a carriage ride, Carpenter asked whether the president had time to view the completed picture. The two walked into the East Room, and the president gazed at himself and his closest associates on a canvas that measured 9 by 15 feet. In Carpenter's words, Lincoln characterized the painting as being as good as it could be, the representation of himself and his colleagues "absolutely perfect."

In this first version of Francis Carpenter's *First Reading of the Emancipation Proclamation,* Lincoln and Seward (seated, second from right) are equally prominent. *Library of Congress*

When Carpenter returned to his studio in New York City, he was a busy man. His White House commission assured him of a stream of paying clients for more traditional portraits. His painting of the Emancipation Proclamation remained on view in the East Room for several months, after which it was sent to Carpenter's studio in New York. Following Lincoln's assassination in April 1865, the painting was exhibited in several major cities. To facilitate transportation, joints were placed in the picture's frame so that it could be folded in half.

For all his political idealism, Carpenter was fully alert to the commercial possibilities of his painting. In 1866 he authorized a copy by engraver Alexander Hay Ritchie, from a miniature painting executed by Carpenter himself. The printer who ran off the engravings later recalled that he could hardly keep up with the orders: "Nearly 30,000 impressions were printed from the steel plate, which is now worn out." Within a few years the Ritchie print was to be found in homes across the North.

Carpenter was still not done with Lincoln. His stay in Washington produced not only a famous painting but also a memoir, one that Carpenter titled *Six Months at the White House with Abraham Lincoln.* Although exact sales figures are not known, the book went through 16 editions and must have turned a nice profit for its author. Carpenter conceded that his book was rambling and episodic; indeed, far too much of it is hearsay, anecdotes of

Lincoln passed on to Carpenter by a variety of the president's associates. But the painter was nothing if not observant, and he appears to have conscientiously recorded what he saw in the Lincoln White House. He is the sole source for some stories, such as that of Lincoln's response to a clergyman who expressed the hope that the Lord was on "our side." Lincoln, in reply, expressed the hope that the nation "should be on the Lord's side." Only Carpenter mentions Lincoln's reported wish that every Wall Street gold speculator should have "his devilish head shot off." Several stories related to Lincoln's reading habits—he once told Carpenter that he had never read a novel to the end—are found only in *Six Months at the White House*.

Although Carpenter's treatment of Lincoln bordered on the reverent, he managed to attract the ire of the president's widow. Irritated by Carpenter's claim to a close relationship with the president, Mrs. Lincoln announced in 1867 that the artist had had fewer than a dozen interviews with her husband, and that he had "intruded frequently into Mr. Lincoln's office, when time was too precious to be idled."

Meanwhile, Carpenter's painting was generating mixed reviews among Lincoln's erstwhile associates. In particular, the central position afforded Secretary Seward offended the secretary of state's many enemies. Hiram Barney, a long time Lincoln associate, complained to Secretary of the Navy Gideon Welles that the painting made it appear that Seward had just finished his draft and Lincoln was reading it for the first time. Chief Justice Salmon P. Chase, who had been Lincoln's secretary of the treasury, was similarly unhappy about Seward's prominence. Chase complained that in Carpenter's painting "Seward is talking, while everyone else listens or stares into vacancy."

The years passed and Carpenter's studio continued to prosper. His painting of the signing of the Treaty of Washington, which settled a series of disputes between the United States and Britain, was purchased by Queen Victoria. Eventually, Carpenter moved to New Rochelle, New York, where he assisted many younger artists. He never attempted another book, but occasionally contributed articles and interviews to various journals.

In 1878 he sold *The First Reading of the Emancipation Proclamation* to Elizabeth Thompson, who, as noted earlier, presented it to the U.S. Capitol, where it hangs today. When the painting was unveiled, however, there had been some subtle changes. The pen that for years had lain near Seward's hand is now held by Lincoln. A lightening of the background behind the president lends a haloed effect. The draft of the Emancipation Proclamation is in Lincoln's hand for all to see, and he is no longer making eye contact with Seward, as in the Ritchie engraving.

It is the Ritchie engraving, however, that appears in many books dealing with the Civil War period. Both versions, despite a certain stodginess, retain their dramatic appeal. Reporter Noah Brooks, a friend of both Lincoln and

By the time Carpenter's painting was hung in the Capitol, Lincoln had been made the central figure. *Author's Collection*

Carpenter, called Carpenter's painting one "which will be prized in every liberty-loving household as a work of art, a group of faithful likenesses of the President and his Cabinet, and as a perpetual remembrance of the noblest event in American history."

CHAPTER 16

Folly at the Crater

IF EVER THERE WAS a hard-luck army among Lincoln's legions in the Civil War, it was that most visible of units, the Army of the Potomac. Almost from the first it had faced the ablest of the Confederate commanders—men of the caliber of Lee, Jackson, and Stuart. It had confronted the most daunting of challenges, capture of the enemy's capital. And then there was the quality of its own commanders. Billy Yank had been led by the likes of Irwin McDowell, George McClellan, Joe Hooker, and Ambrose E. Burnside. Small wonder that the Army of the Potomac began its 1864 campaign against Richmond with some foreboding.

But there were positive signs as well. In recognition that defeat of Lee's army would effectively end the war, the North was sparing nothing to assure the success of the campaign. Although the Army of the Potomac remained under the nominal command of Gen. George G. Meade, the commanding general, Ulysses S. Grant, traveled with Meade's army in this latest Virginia campaign. Beginning in April, the spring offensive took on the aspect of a continuous battle, with the 100,000-man Army of the Potomac moving inexorably south. But somehow Robert E. Lee managed to keep his Army of Northern Virginia between Grant and the Confederate capital.

In one of his more skillful moves, Grant succeeded in stealing a march on Lee in mid-June, moving the bulk of his force from northeast of Richmond to positions south of the James River. But the Army of the Potomac's bad luck held. Grant's plan had called for an attack on the railroad junction at Petersburg, 23 miles south of Richmond, with a view to cutting supplies to the capital. The movement went smoothly, and as dawn broke on June 16 the Federals had a good portion of Gen. "Baldy" Smith's corps within sight of Petersburg, where Confederate Gen. P. G. T. Beauregard could muster only 3,000 defenders. But a combination of delays, bad maps, and imprecise orders on the Federal side enabled Beauregard to reinforce his lines until Lee could arrive with the main army. Grant, frustrated, returned to his cigars. Petersburg would have to be taken by siege.

The threat that Grant posed to Richmond and Petersburg was obvious, and Lee's army was in dire straits. At the same time, living conditions were almost as onerous for the Federals as for the Confederates. The summer dust lay inches deep—there had been no rain for weeks—and one New York soldier concluded that the combination of dust and heat was killing more men than the Johnnies. An artilleryman quipped that one jumping grasshopper raised so much dust that the Rebels thought that Grant was moving again.[1]

One of the regiments in Gen. Ambrose E. Burnside's IX Corps included a large number of one-time coal miners from Schuylkill County, Pennsylvania. Its commanding officer, 31-year-old Henry Pleasants, was an engineer who had worked for the Pennsylvania Railroad in the 1850s and had helped drill a 4,200-foot tunnel through the Alleghenies. One day late in June, Pleasants assembled his officers in an underground room near the front. "That God-damned fort is the only thing between us and Petersburg," he told them, adding, "I have an idea we can blow it up."[2] Pleasants put his thoughts on paper and sent them up the chain of command. A few days later his division commander, Brig. Gen. Robert Potter, told Pleasants that the two of them had an appointment with the corps commander, General Burnside.

The 40-year-old Burnside was one of a number of senior generals on the Federal side who had graduated from West Point and then gone on to civil careers. After returning to service following the attack on Fort Sumter, he had led a successful operation against the North Carolina coast in 1862 and emerged as one of the army's more popular corps commanders. Burnside was modest and he took care of his troops. One soldier wrote that the men were always ready to cheer Burnside's "manly countenance, bald head and unmistakable whiskers"—mutton-chop adornments that would enter the lexicon as *sideburns*, and become a more permanent legacy than anything Burnside achieved on the battlefield.

In contrast to the soldiers of his IX Corps, many Federal officers did not hold Burnside in high esteem. In a brief stint as commander of the Army of the Potomac he had almost destroyed it in a frontal attack against Lee at Fredericksburg. Demoted to corps command, Burnside remained a soldier of modest capabilities, one who had to be kept under constant supervision.

Whatever his other shortcomings, Burnside was open to innovation, as Potter and Pleasants discovered that June evening. It was sweltering in Burnside's tent, but the corps commander put the two men at ease and listened to what Pleasants proposed: a tunnel under the Rebel lines, to be filled with explosives and detonated to breach Lee's defenses. With such a breakthrough, the war could be brought to a speedy close! Burnside was impressed. He would have to take it up with Meade, but he told Pleasants to get his men to work on it. No great thought went into where the tunnel should best be dug; it was Pleasants's idea, and it would be done on his section of the line, which was only about 130 yards from the Rebel defenses.

Burnside's immediate superior was the commander of the Army of the Potomac, Meade, whose normal irascibility was aggravated by the fact that he now had Grant looking over his shoulder. Meade indicated from the outset that he had no confidence in the mining scheme, but, doubtless influenced by Grant, he allowed the project to go forward. The idea of a protracted siege was no more appealing to Grant that it was to his soldiers, and the commanding general listened attentively to Pleasants's plan, which held out the promise of breaching Lee's defenses and assuring the capture of Petersburg.

Digging began on June 25. The Confederate line ran roughly parallel to and east of the Jerusalem Plank Road. The land was gently rolling and relatively clear; no one worried too much about the fact that there was a distinct elevation behind the Confederate works that might assist Rebel defenders.

Pleasants was beset with problems from the outset, and his later testimony before a congressional committee only hints at what must have been daily frustrations. He had to dispose of the dirt removed from the mine, but no one was very helpful; ultimately, he was reduced to requisitioning old cracker boxes. His requests for special tools were ignored, even though the project had all the requisite approvals.[3]

One particular problem vexed Pleasants: He had to establish the depth and direction of the shaft to assure that the eventual explosion would inflict serious damage. Once again, he was at the mercy of the army bureaucracy:

> I wanted an accurate instrument with which to make the necessary triangulations. I had to make them on the farthest front line, where the enemy's sharp-shooters could reach me. I could not get the instrument I wanted, although there was one at army headquarters, and General Burnside had to send to Washington and get an old-fashioned theodite, which was given to me. . . . General Burnside told me that General Meade and Major Duane, chief engineer of the Army of the Potomac, said the thing could not be done—that it was all clap-trap and nonsense; that such a length of mine had never been excavated in military operations, and could not be; that I would either get the men smothered, for want of air, or crushed by the falling of the earth.[4]

A less determined man might have given up, but Pleasants persisted. An air shaft just inside the Federal lines alleviated the ventilation problem and the cracker boxes proved effective in moving dirt out of the cramped, five-foot-high tunnel. Within four weeks Pleasants's soldier-miners had constructed a

510-foot shaft that terminated like a T in a horizontal gallery 75 feet across. On July 23 the Pennsylvanians began placing 320 twenty-five-pound kegs of powder in the tunnel, most of it in the horizontal gallery. Pleasants had asked for 560 kegs, but the charge was reduced on Meade's order.

The Confederates, however, would not be caught by surprise. Although the Federals maintained reasonably good security, the Rebels learned, probably from deserters, that something was up. Col. Charles Wainwright, chief of artillery in Warren's corps, wrote in his diary on July 21 that Rebel pickets were making good-humored inquiries about "Burnside's mine." Their commanders took the threat seriously and initiated countermining to locate the Yankee tunnel. By July 21, Confederate sappers insisted that they could hear the picks and shovels of their Federal counterparts.[5] Confederate suspicions were well founded, but their options were limited. Because they could not simply abandon their lines, the initiative remained with the Federals.

On July 26, Burnside submitted his plan of attack. He argued that, although the Rebels were aware of the tunneling, they did not know the location of the tunnel or the scope of the proposed explosion. Time was of the essence, however; the mine should be exploded and an attack made within the next two or three days. The assault should take place before dawn, with the lead division drawn up in formation before the mine was exploded. Each column should include engineers to remove obstructions. In Burnside's judgment, "Our chances for success, in a plan of this kind, are more than even."[6] Grant agreed. In a feint to draw troops away from the Petersburg defenses, Grant ordered Hancock's II Corps, supported by cavalry, to make a diversionary thrust north of the James. Hancock began his move on July 26.

Meanwhile, Burnside was not idle. A recent addition to his corps was a division of black troops, commanded by Gen. Edward Ferrero and staffed primarily by white officers. Burnside planned to use his entire corps in the attack but he wanted Ferrero's division—which had seen little action, in contrast to his other depleted divisions—to lead. In the hot days of mid-July, Ferrero drilled his division in advancing along a narrow front and in deploying along both sides of what the Federals expected to be a very large crater.

It was here that things began to go wrong. On the afternoon before the attack, Meade told Burnside that Ferrero's division could not lead the advance. The entire operation was something of a gamble, and it should not be led by troops that had never been under fire. Burnside remonstrated, pointing out that Ferrero's division was his freshest and had been receiving special training. When Burnside appealed to Grant, the commanding general sided with Meade; the battle must be spearheaded by one of the white divisions, with Ferrero in support. Both Meade and Grant were conscious that if anything went wrong and Ferrero's division incurred heavy casualties, the generals would be vulnerable to charges of having callously sacrificed their black soldiers.

This crucial decision came on July 29, just 12 hours before the scheduled detonation of the mine. Burnside swallowed his annoyance and met that afternoon with the commanders of his three white divisions. Gen. Robert B. Potter, under whom Pleasants served, was a capable commander with a good record. A second division was commanded by Gen. Orlando B. Willcox, a solid professional who had been with the Army of the Potomac since Antietam. The third and most junior division commander was Gen. James H. Ledlie, a civil engineer before the war, who had led a New York artillery regiment but had only recently been promoted to division command. His division, composed largely of artillery and dismounted cavalry, was much the weakest in the IX Corps. Burnside himself had recently said of Ledlie's division, "They are worthless. They didn't enlist to fight. . . ."[7]

As Bruce Catton has noted, the Army of the Potomac had a good many incompetent generals but not many who were cowards. Ledlie was one of the few. In the attack before Petersburg on June 18, Ledlie had taken to the bottle and at the climax of the battle was far to the rear, heavily in his cups. This was embarrassing to the division, and Ledlie's staff appear to have kept this information from Burnside. Even so, the corps commander's behavior at this final conference before the battle bordered on the bizarre. Burnside had always liked to gamble; as a junior officer en route to a prewar posting, he had once gambled away his travel advance and had been obliged to borrow funds from a Louisville merchant. Now, in conference with Potter, Willcox, and Ledlie, Burnside declined to decide which unit should lead the advance, suggesting instead that his division commanders draw lots. The short straw, in vindication of Murphy's Law, went to Ledlie.

The final orders called for Ledlie's division to lead the advance through the enemy's works—or what remained of them—and thence to Cemetery Hill, about 400 yards behind the Confederate works. Ledlie was to be followed by Willcox and Potter in that order; Ferrero's would be the fourth and last division to advance. If all went well, Burnside's attack would be exploited by Ord's and Warren's corps. Earlier, Burnside had emphasized the importance of skirting the crater. Now, on the eve of the attack, the emphasis was on capturing Cemetery Hill, which was seen as the main objective. Hancock's diversionary attack had forced Lee to withdraw several divisions from the Petersburg front, and Federal prospects seemed bright.

Shortly after midnight on July 30, Burnside's divisions were in position. Few of the Federal soldiers had slept, for word passed through the ranks that the long-rumored mine was about to go off. Three o'clock came and went, with much shuffling and glancing at watches. Pleasants lit the fuse at 3:15 A.M., but a half-hour passed without any explosion. At about 4:00, Pleasants directed Sgt. Harry Reese, a one-time mine boss, to investigate the delay. In one of the more nerve-wracking episodes of the day, Reese, accompanied by

Lt. Jacob Douty, entered the shaft, where they found that the fuse had died at the first splicing. Reese re-ignited the fuse and led a very rapid exit.

Lt. Joseph Scroggs, an officer in Ferrero's division, wrote in his diary that the suspense had become painful when, at 4:45 A.M., the mine finally detonated. Involving as it did 8,000 pounds of powder, it may have been the greatest man-made explosion up to that time. To men near the front, the blast seemed in slow motion: first a long, deep rumble, then a swelling of the ground and a great rising. In Scroggs's words, "The earth shook and quivered under our feet . . . lifting the rebel fort with guns and garrison high in the air."[8] Maj. William Powell of Ledlie's division remembered it as "a magnificent spectacle . . . as the mass of earth went up into the air, carrying with it men, guns, carriages and timbers."[9] Still another soldier felt it as "a heavy shaking of the earth, with a rumbling, muffled sound."[10]

The men of Ledlie's division were struck dumb by what they had just seen. A few headed for the rear. For at least 10 minutes no one heeded the order to advance, in part because a great cloud of dust obscured what was left of the Rebel entrenchments. In the wake of the exploding mine, carefully placed Federal artillery—a total of 110 guns and 55 mortars—opened a thunderous barrage at Confederate defenses on either side of the crater. Then Ledlie's advance brigade, commanded by Col. E. G. Marshall, discovered a problem. Despite Burnside's orders, nothing had been done to remove defensive obstructions from in front of the Federals' own lines. The troops hacked out a narrow passage through the Union abatis—a maze of sharpened tree limbs—and clambered through and over the empty trenches that lay between the two lines. In the process, however, all semblance of formation was lost.

Some 130 yards ahead was the crater—about 60 feet wide, 170 feet long, and 30 feet deep. The area was littered with guns, bodies, and timbers; a Rebel artilleryman who had been completely buried except for his legs told his captors that he had been asleep at the time of the explosion and had awakened to find himself flying through the air. Twenty minutes after the explosion the men of Marshall's brigade were still staring in wonder at the smoldering crater, but they were soon pressed into it by the advance of those behind them.

Meanwhile, the Confederates were pulling themselves together. The timing of the blast had taken them by surprise, but they had known that something was brewing and were quick to respond. They had lost nearly 300 men in the explosion, and the Federal artillery barrage that ensued had emptied Confederate trenches adjacent to the crater. But with the Federal attack slowed, Confederate artillery began to range on the crater. From Cemetery Hill came the rattle of Rebel musketry.

In the crater, a handful of Union officers yelled themselves hoarse trying to get soldiers out of the hole and on with the attack. Ledlie, of course, was nowhere to be found; he was, in fact, in a bombproof trench well within Federal lines, drinking rum supplied by a division surgeon. From time to time he would dispatch a messenger, ordering an advance toward the crest of the ridge. With the day's first light, Potter's and Willcox's divisions continued to use one narrow corridor to join the attack. Reinforcements were told to deploy into the deserted Confederate trenches on either side of the crater, but the number of soldiers in "the hole" continued to increase.

Meade had believed from the outset that if the attack was to succeed it would have to do so in the first rush. But the period of about 30 minutes when Cemetery Hill was there for the taking was now gone. Between the crater and Cemetery Hill was a small ravine, and the Confederate commander, Gen. William Malone, put troops into it. By 6:00 A.M. fire from the ravine was heavy. Rebel artillery also began to make itself felt. A four-gun Confederate battery north of the crater directed canister into the Yankees who were attempting to advance from the captured entrenchments. Federal artillery silenced several guns but could not put the battery out of action. The Rebels also had 16 guns along the Jerusalem Plank Road, and as the July sun rose these began to do heavy execution.

By 6:30 A.M. it was clear that Cemetery Hill was not going to be taken easily and might not be taken at all. But the attackers had no backup plan in case their initial rush failed. Burnside, from his command post a quarter-mile behind the Federal lines, continued to pour in his divisions, who pressed those in front of them into the crater where the steep walls made any further advance difficult. Gen. Edward Ord tried to advance his corps in support of Burnside but found the way jammed. At 7:20 Burnside advised Meade by field telegraph that he was doing all he could to move his men forward but that the advance was difficult. When Meade asked angrily what was going on, Burnside wired back that Meade's communication was "unofficer-like and ungentlemanly."[11]

Ferrero's division had begun its advance at about 7:00. His black soldiers marched past the white troops of Ord's corps, but Ferrero insisted on confirming with Burnside that he was still expected to add his troops to the maelstrom in the Confederate lines. Offered a chance to cut his losses, Burnside passed up the opportunity, telling Ferrero that Cemetery Hill remained his objective. Ferrero ordered his division into battle while he himself stopped in Ledlie's dugout for a drink. Brigade and regimental commanders led the black soldiers into battle, moving around the southern lip of the crater. "The fire upon them was incessant and severe," wrote Major Powell of Ledlie's staff, "and many acts of personal heroism were done here by officers and men." Powell related how one black sergeant spotted one of his men attempting to take shelter in the crater. "None of your damn skulkin'!" the sergeant cried, and, lifting the soldier by the waistband of his trousers, carried him to the crest of the crater, pushed him out, and quickly followed.[12]

Eventually, elements of three black regiments—perhaps 200 men—reached the little ravine from which the Confederates had been aiming such destructive fire. But the Rebels charged, and when the smoke had cleared most bluecoats were running desperately for cover with enraged Southern infantry at their heels. To most Confederates the North's employment of black troops was nothing short of infamous, and at the crater no quarter was given.

At about 9:30 Meade ordered the withdrawal of all troops. This was easier said than done, for Confederate mortars by now were pouring a deadly fire into the crater, where the Federals were packed so closely together that many could not use their weapons. As the sun rose higher, it beat down relentlessly on the wounded. Lt. Freeman S. Bowley later recalled,

> With a dozen of my own company I went down the traverse to the Crater. . . . A full line around the crest of the Crater were loading and firing as fast as they could, and the men were dropping thick and fast, most of them shot through the head. . . . The day was fearfully hot; the wounded were crying for water, and the canteens were empty. . . . At 11 o'clock a determined charge was made by the enemy; we repulsed it, but when the fire slackened the ammunition was fearfully low.[13]

Federal soldiers, in growing numbers, attempted to make their way back to their own lines but suffered heavy casualties. Shortly after noon the Confederates of Mahone's division charged the crater once again. Some bluecoats remembered cries of "Take the white man—kill the nigger."[14] A Southern journalist who viewed the crater later that day called it the most horrible sight he had ever seen. "The sides and bottom of the chasm were literally lined with Yankee dead," he wrote. "Some had evidently been killed with the butts of muskets as their crushed skulls and badly mashed faces too plainly indicated."[15]

By one o'clock the battle was over. Grant was disgusted; he telegraphed General Halleck in Washington that the debacle at the crater was "the saddest affair I have witnessed in the war. Such opportunity for carrying fortifications I have never seen and do not expect again to have."[16] Two decades later, in his memoirs, Grant called the effort "a stupendous failure," one that had resulted from "inefficiency on the part of the corps commander [Burnside] and the incompetency of the division commander [Ledlie] who was sent to lead the assault."[17]

Burnside had much to account for. Not only had he determined his order of battle by lot, but he had failed to assure that Federal defenses were cleared to facilitate the advance, and he had continued to move reinforcements into the battle after it was obvious that the crater was a death trap. In General

Ord's later testimony, the soldiers in the crater "were about as much use there as so many men at the bottom of a well."[18]

But not all the onus belonged on Burnside. Grant and Meade made inexcusable errors. When Pleasants proposed the use of a mine, neither Grant nor Meade took any special interest, and Pleasants was left to pursue his plan in an area of the line where the topography would favor the defenders once the mine had exploded. Meade's arbitrary reduction in the size of the powder charge from 14,000 pounds to 8,000 pounds does not appear to have influenced the outcome but was nonetheless capricious. Then, of course, there was the question of which division should lead the advance. Although there may have been some justification for not putting a black division in the van, Meade was culpable for having altered his order of battle only hours before the mine was to explode.

Union casualties at the crater were about 3,800—more than a third of them from Ferrero's division—compared with about 1,500 for the Confederates. The battle was not a major engagement in terms of the number of troops involved, but in strategic terms it represented Grant's last chance to gain Petersburg without a long and costly siege. The city would remain in Confederate hands until April 3, 1865, when Lee was at last compelled to abandon both Richmond and Petersburg.

There was no absence of recrimination among the Federal commanders. Horace Porter, an officer on Grant's staff, witnessed a shouting match between Meade and Burnside which, to Porter, "went far toward confirming one's belief in the wealth and flexibility of the English language as a medium of personal dispute."[19] The ax, however, fell selectively. Grant was held in such high esteem that Lincoln never considered replacing him. Others were less fortunate. Ledlie was dismissed in disgrace, and Ferrero was transferred to Gen. Benjamin F. Butler's Army of the James. Meade wanted to court-martial Burnside, but Grant demurred; he ordered instead a court of inquiry, whose report was sufficiently damaging that Burnside requested a leave of absence from which he never returned to active service.

At the outset of the war both armies had their share of incompetents like Ledlie, Burnside, and Ferrero. But most such officers were weeded out in the first year of the fighting, and it is a reflection on the Federal high command that such bunglers remained in responsible commands in the fourth year of the war. The final word on the battle of the crater may have been the judgment by Union Col. Charles Wainwright, who wrote of his superiors, "Surely such a lot of fools did not deserve to succeed."[20]

CHAPTER 17

The Man in the Gray Overcoat

SECRETARY OF STATE William Henry Seward had a habit, when things were going well, of softly rubbing has palms together. In the early months of 1865, with Lincoln reelected and the war nearly won, Seward was rubbing his palms together a great deal. Except for the continuing French presence in Mexico, the country's foreign relations were more stable than any time since 1861.

Relations within Lincoln's cabinet also were smoother on the eve of victory than in the anxious months of 1851 and 1862. Seward and Secretary of the Navy Gideon Welles were the only holdovers from among Lincoln's initial appointments. Although Seward's relations with the acerbic Welles would never be warm, both men had made an effort to reduce friction. The secretary of war, Edwin Stanton, no longer felt beholden to Seward for his appointment, and his political views were closer to those of the Radicals in Congress than to Lincoln's and Seward's. But their personal relations were amicable; Seward was prone to refer to Stanton as the organizer of victory.

The spring of 1865 found Seward surrounded as usual by family and friends. His invalid wife, however, was not among them; after a visit to Washington in December 1864 Frances Seward had retreated to her home in Auburn, New York, which she greatly preferred to Washington. But the secretary did not lack for companionship; he shared his house on the corner of Lafayette Park—known to Washingtonians as the Old Clubhouse—with his older son, Gus, an army officer; his second son, Frederick, a valued assistant in the State Department; and his 20-year-old daughter, Fanny.

Young Fanny had spent most of the war years with her mother in Auburn. In the autumn of 1864, however, over her mother's objections, she had moved to Washington to be near her father. Her health was fragile, and she was subject to colds. But she made her debut in Washington and enjoyed life in the wartime capital. It appeared for a time that one of President

122

Lincoln's secretaries, John Nicolay, was interested in Fanny, but romance never bloomed.

Richmond fell on April 3, 1865. Lincoln went there to sit in Jefferson Davis's chair in the Confederate White House, while Stanton ordered an 800-gun salute in Washington. In Lincoln's absence revelers gathered at the State Department, where they found Seward in an equally festive mood. He whimsically promised to tell Lord John Russell, the British foreign secretary, that British merchants would find cotton legally exported from the United States cheaper than cotton smuggled through the blockade.

The last thing that worried Seward in this festive time was the danger of assassination. He had, of course, been the target of many threats, in part because he had been a prominent antislavery spokesman long before the emergence of Lincoln. But as secretary of state he had been largely out of the public eye. When John Bigelow, an American diplomat in Paris, had warned of an alleged plot against Lincoln and his cabinet, Seward was unimpressed. He wrote in reply that assassination was foreign to America, a practice "so vicious and desperate" that it could never become part of the American political system. He noted how the president, in warm weather, rode two or three miles from the White House to the Soldiers' Home unguarded. So did Seward. "I go there unattended at all hours, by daylight and by moonlight, by starlight and without any light."[1]

The warm afternoon on April 5 was a harbinger of spring. Seward left the State Department early, having planned a carriage ride with Fred, Fanny, and a friend of his daughter named Mary Titus. Some distance out Vermont Avenue one of the doors of the carriage refused to stay closed, and the coachman, Henry Key, stopped to make repairs. As he did so, the horses bolted and turned for home. Fred, outside the coach, tried unsuccessfully to control the team. As the carriage picked up speed, Seward, over Fanny's protests, attempted to gather the reins. He fell heavily from the coach, which careened back toward Lafayette Park until the exhausted horses found refuge in an alley.

When help reached Seward, he was unconscious. He was moved carefully back to his house, where he was treated by an Army surgeon, Maj. Basil Norris, and then by the family physician, Dr. Tullio Verdi. The injuries were serious. Seward's face was bruised and swollen and he appeared to have suffered a concussion. His right shoulder was dislocated and his right arm broken. His jaw was fractured on both sides. When Seward regained consciousness that evening he was in severe pain.

The family informed his wife by telegraph. Frances came to Washington the following day. "I find Henry worse than I had anticipated," she wrote her sister. "It makes my heart ache to look at him."[2] The doctors expected a full recovery, but setting the patient's jaw and shoulder was an ordeal. At times Seward was delirious. To assist the family and house staff and to act as nurse,

Stanton provided a convalescent soldier, George Robinson. The assignment would make Robinson a celebrity.

There were many callers at the Old Clubhouse, but few were admitted to the sickroom. Among the most frequent visitors was the gruff Stanton. Another was President Lincoln. The president had been in City Point, Virginia, when he heard of Seward's accident. Then came the long-awaited news of Lee's surrender. Amid the bells and salutes and rejoicing, Lincoln decided that he would return to Washington. Frederick Seward later described the president's call on his father:

> "You are back from Richmond?" whispered Seward, who was hardly able to articulate.
>
> "Yes," said Lincoln, "and I think we are near the end, at last."
>
> Then leaning his tall form across the bed, and resting on his elbow, so as to bring his face close to that of the wounded man, he gave him an account of his experiences "at the front". . . . They were left together for half an hour or more. Then the door opened softly, and Mr. Lincoln came out gently, intimating by a silent look and gesture that Seward had fallen into a feverish slumber. . . . It was their last meeting.[3]

John Wilkes Booth was a promising 26-year-old actor who, although strongly sympathetic to the South, had never quite gotten around to serving in the Confederate army. Seeking some dramatic means of giving expression to his sympathies, Booth, in about September 1864, formulated a plan to kidnap President Lincoln on some occasion when the president was riding to or from the Soldiers' Home.

In November, Booth took up residence at the National Hotel and began implementing his scheme. His first recruits were two high school chums, Samuel Arnold and Michael O'Laughlin. Washington still had more than its share of disgruntled secessionists, and Booth soon added three other kindred spirits—John Surratt, David Herold, and George Atzerodt—to his band. Booth's headquarters was Mary Surratt's boardinghouse on H Street. His prize recruit was one Lewis Thornton Powell, who would later be known by the alias Lewis Paine.

The son of a Baptist clergyman, Powell was helping to run his father's farm in Florida when the Civil War erupted. With his strapping physique, "unflinching dark gray eyes," and a "stolid, remorseless expression," Powell was a natural for the Confederate army. Assigned to a Florida regiment, he fought at Antietam and Chancellorsville, but was wounded at Gettysburg and taken prisoner. While serving as a nurse in a Baltimore hospital he

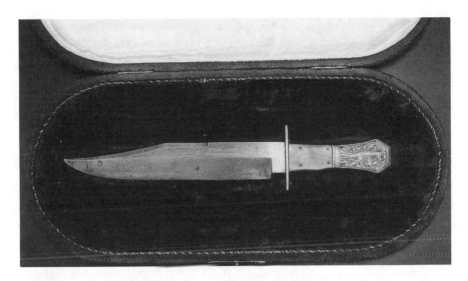

The Bowie knife with which Powell attacked Seward. *John K. Lattimer Collection*

escaped and joined the Confederate rangers of Col. John S. Mosby, in northern Virginia. Brutalized by the war yet despairing of the Confederate cause, Powell surrendered in January 1865, giving his name as Paine, perhaps to cover the fact of his earlier escape.

"Paine" returned to Baltimore, where he boarded with the family of a nurse-acquaintance, Maggie Branson. While there, he was reported to military authorities for having assaulted a black maid who had "called him some names." According to later testimony, Paine then attacked her; "he threw her on the ground and stamped on her body, struck her on the forehead, and said he would kill her."[4] Paine was arrested, but on the trial date several witnesses failed to appear. The provost marshal released Paine after administering an oath of allegiance and ordering him to remain north of Philadelphia for the duration of the war.

Paine would later testify that he had first seen John Wilkes Booth in Richmond, where Booth was appearing in a play. Paine had subsequently sought out the actor, and the two were soon on friendly terms. There is some question as to whether Booth performed in Richmond at the time indicated, but he does appear to have known Paine and to have encountered him in Baltimore in March 1865. Paine, unemployed, was an easy recruit for "Captain Booth," as Paine called him. Booth put him up at the Herndon House at Ninth and H streets, close to Mrs. Surratt's.

Time had run out on Booth's kidnapping scheme. The Confederacy was in its last throes, and Lincoln was not yet visiting his cottage at the Soldiers' Home. Arnold and O'Laughlin had backed out of the kidnapping scheme.

Booth, who was drinking heavily, apparently decided at this time to attempt to kill Lincoln and prominent members of his administration. Although he may have hoped that the resulting turmoil would revive the Confederacy, his primary motive appears to have been vengeance. Booth made his new plans on April 14, assigning to George Atzerodt the task of murdering Vice President Andrew Johnson, and to Paine the killing of Seward.

Almost immediately Booth's improvised plans went awry. Atzerodt decided that kidnapping was one thing, murder was another; after reflecting in a hotel bar, he determined to make no move against Johnson. But Paine, the good soldier, proceeded to carry out Booth's command. Because Paine was not familiar with Washington, David Herold showed him the way to Seward's residence. At about 10 o'clock on the evening of April 14, Seward had fallen into an uneasy slumber in his third-floor bedroom when the front doorbell rang. One of the servants, 19-year-old William Bell, opened the door. A man in a gray overcoat said that he had some medicine from Dr. Verdi for Secretary Seward. Bell responded that no one was allowed upstairs, but the stranger insisted that he was to deliver the medicine in person. Bell led the stranger to the third landing, where they encountered Fred Seward.

Paine repeated his story to Fred, who was initially unsuspecting. His father might be sleeping, he replied, but he would go see. Fred went to the front of the house, to the last door on the left. In a moment he was back. His father was indeed asleep, he said, asking Paine for the package. The stranger demurred; he *had* to deliver the medicine in person. Frederick Seward began to lose patience. He would take responsibility for the "medicine"; Dr. Verdi would not blame his messenger if the family denied him admittance.

Paine hesitated, mumbled something, and turned as if to start back down the stairs. He then reached into his coat, pulled out a big navy revolver, and attempted to fire at Fred. There was only a click; the gun had misfired.

With two giant strides Paine was on top of Fred, smashing his head with the pistol. Although Fred does not appear to have cried out, the sound of the scuffle carried into the sickroom, where Fanny had been sitting with her father. She was about to turn the bedside watch over to Robinson, the soldier-nurse, when one of them opened the door to check on the commotion. Paine struck at Robinson with his backup weapon, a large Bowie knife, inflicting only a glancing blow to the head but clearing Robinson out of the doorway. He then made directly for the bed at the front of the house.

Paine thus far had played his role to perfection, locating his victim and refusing to be deterred by either Fred Seward or Robinson. Now, in the dim light of the sickroom, his luck ran out. Seward was on the side of the bed away from the door, reclining against a frame designed to provide maximum comfort for his injured shoulder. Unable to use his revolver, Paine slashed repeatedly at Seward's head and neck, but in the dim light his aim was poor. Robinson would recall,

I saw him strike Mr. Seward with the same knife with which he cut my forehead. It was large knife, and he held it with the blade down below his hand. I saw him cut Mr. Seward twice that I am sure of; the first time he struck him on the right cheek, and then he seemed to be cutting around his neck.[5]

By then the courageous Robinson was on him. The soldier suffered a second wound in the shoulder but succeeded in wrestling the assassin off the bed. Gus, aroused by the noise, joined Robinson in attempting to subdue Paine. According to Gus, the intruder shouted, "I'm mad! I'm mad!"

Through the pandemonium, Fanny screamed for help. William Bell, on seeing Paine strike Fred Seward, had gone to an army office next door in

Lewis Powell, alias Lewis Paine, the former Confederate soldier who attempted to murder Secretary of State Seward while John Wilkes Booth assassinated Lincoln.
Louis A. Warren Lincoln Library

search of help. Frances, hearing the noise, emerged from her room at the back of the house but could not comprehend what was happening. Finally, Paine tore himself away from Robinson, struck Gus in the forehead, and bolted down the stairs. Near the front door he encountered a State Department messenger, Emerick Hansell, just mounting the stairs. Paine stabbed Hansell and rushed on to where he had left his horse, dropping the knife as he ran.

The assaults on Lincoln and Seward occurred within minutes of one another, and many people heard of the attack on Seward first. Stanton was at home undressing, having spoken briefly to some serenaders, when his wife called from downstairs, "Mr. Seward is murdered!" "Humbug," Stanton replied, "I left him only an hour ago." But the secretary of war pulled on his clothes again, questioned his wife's informant, and hurried over to the Old Clubhouse.[6]

The story was much the same with Gideon Welles. The navy secretary was asleep when a messenger arrived with word of the assaults on both Lincoln and Seward. "Damn the Rebels, this is their work," he remarked, hurrying to Lafayette Park. There was a dense crowd around the Seward residence—soldiers, onlookers, and diplomats in formal dress from a party nearby. Welles pushed his way through the crowd until he spotted Stanton. The two cabinet officers were allowed up the blood-splattered staircase, where they learned that both Seward and Fred were seriously injured. Stanton ordered a guard put in front of the house; he and Welles then went to Ford's Theatre, the scene of a still greater tragedy.

Once Paine had fled, the occupants of the house turned their attention to the injured. Poor Fanny would long remember the blood: "My dress was stained with it—Mother's was dabbled with it—it was on everything."[7] No other American assassin had injured so many people in a single attack as had Paine. In the course of about three minutes he had inflicted serious injuries on Secretary Seward and Fred; had given Hansell, the messenger, a deep wound in his side; and had inflicted less serious injuries on Robinson and Gus Seward. Robinson ministered immediately to Secretary Seward, who was on the floor alongside his bed, wrapped in bloody sheets like some latter-day Julius Caesar. At first Robinson feared the worst. Then he detected a pulse. Seward opened his eyes and whispered that Robinson should send for a surgeon and the police, then lock up the house. Later, Seward would say that Paine's blade felt cold, and that he had felt what seemed like rain streaming down his neck. Whether he was thrown off the bed by the impetus of Paine's blows or whether he rolled off instinctively is unclear.

The first physician to arrive was Dr. Verdi, who found his patient back on his bed where Robinson had laid him, bleeding profusely. Verdi feared that the jugular vein had been severed, but when this proved not to be the case he checked the bleeding with ice water. Verdi assured the family that the secretary's wounds were not fatal, "upon which Mr. Seward stretched out his hands and received his family."[8] Soon Dr. Norris, who had treated Seward's earlier injuries, arrived, followed by the surgeon general, Dr. Joseph Barnes. Norris sutured Seward's torn cheeks without benefit of anesthetic, but the patient later maintained that the process had not been especially painful.

Seward's narrow escape appeared to have resulted from several factors: the failure of Paine's revolver, which forced him to resort to the uncertainties of assassination by knife; the dim light in the sickroom, which may have disoriented the intruder; and Robinson's courageous intervention. Contemporary accounts refer to Seward's having worn a cervical collar that deflected the assassin's knife, but recent scholarship has raised doubts as to whether Seward was wearing any such device.

Ironically, the most seriously injured of those in the Old Clubhouse was Fred. The blows from Paine's defective revolver had fractured his skull, exposing the brain in two places. Within an hour after the attack he was unable to speak; helped to bed, he became comatose and remained so for several days. It was a full month before he was judged to be out of danger.

Early the next morning, after a sleepless night, Frances told her husband of the events at Ford's Theatre. She said simply, "Henry, the president is gone."[9] Seward seemed to understand. The fact that he was promptly told of Lincoln's death discredits a story that enjoyed a considerable vogue at that time. In this version, word of the president's death was initially withheld from the secretary lest he be further upset. But within days of Paine's attack, he asked to be moved so as to view the spring foliage from his window. On noting the flags on government buildings at half-staff, Seward announced that the president was dead. To an attendant's faltering denial Seward reportedly responded, "If he had been alive, he would have been the first to call on me, but he has not been here."[10]

Seward began a slow recovery. For weeks he suffered from double vision. Because of his broken jaw and lacerated cheeks he could not speak without pain, and communicated by writing on a slate. When social reformer Dorothea Dix sent him an exotic dish involving eggs and wine, Fanny asked him whether he liked it. "I like it because I like Miss Dix," Seward scrawled.[11] By April 19 the patient was able to sit up and watch Lincoln's funeral cortege as it left the White House. President Johnson and his cabinet called at the Old Clubhouse on May 9, and Seward was able to receive them in the parlor, although his jaw was secured by an iron frame that made it virtually impossible to talk.

As long as Fred was in danger, his mother hovered by his bedside. But as the Seward men improved, Frances herself went into a decline. By late May she was bedridden, and on June 21, nine weeks after Paine's assault, she died. Most Americans attributed her death to anxiety growing out of the attack on her family.

Paine's period of freedom after his assault on Seward was brief. Booth had provided no escape plan for his confederate, and two days after the carnage of April 14 Paine showed up at the Surratt boardinghouse professing to be a laborer in search of work. Mrs. Surratt denied knowing him, but he was arrested on suspicion. Once he was identified as Seward's assailant, Paine was put in irons; 10 men later divided a $5,000 reward for his capture.

Booth was tracked to the Garrett farm in northern Virginia, where he was killed by Federal soldiers on April 26. Five days later President Johnson ordered the remaining conspirators tried by a military commission—a decision that, because civil courts were open and available, was of dubious constitutionality. Gen. William E. Doster, who defended Paine before the nine-man military commission at Washington Barracks, attempted an insanity defense, but the death of Frances Seward in the wake of the assault on her family made a successful defense of Paine on any grounds a formidable task. Reporter Noah Brooks observed Paine closely, writing that "he sits bolt upright against the wall, looming like a young giant above the others." Brooks thought he detected a gleam in the assailant's eyes when the prosecution introduced the knife with which he had carried out his assault, a heavy, horn-handled weapon with a double-edged blade at the point.[12]

Paine denied nothing at his trial and appeared indifferent to his fate. One of the judges was heard to remark that because Paine seemed to want to be hanged, the commission might as well accommodate him. He was sentenced to death on June 30, along with Atzerodt, Herold, and Mrs. Surratt. Paine was uncommunicative almost to the end, but ultimately told Doster that he regretted the injury he had done to Fred Seward. The four convicted conspirators died on the gallows at Washington Barracks on July 7.

Over the years, scholars and assassination buffs have occasionally asked the question, Why Seward? That Andrew Johnson was on Booth's list was understandable—he was both vice president and a "renegade" Southerner—but had Seward done more to bring down the Confederacy than, say, Stanton or Grant?* None of the conspirators shed any light on this question at the trial.

One school of thought holds that Booth's objective was to produce such chaos in Washington as to permit the Confederacy somehow to fight on. If this had been the case, Seward was a logical target, for he was the best-

*For all Seward's prominence, he did not figure in the presidential succession. Under the relevant statute (twice amended since then) in case of the death of both the president and the vice president, the president of the Senate pro tempore was to act as president until one could be elected.

known member of Lincoln's cabinet. But the bulk of the evidence suggests that Booth was motivated principally by a desire for revenge. In the rambling journal that he penned during his escape, Booth wrote of Lincoln, "Our country owed all her trouble to him." A Union sustained by force "is not what I have loved." He compared himself to Brutus but insisted that he, Booth, was striking down a tyrant greater than Caesar.[13]

If Lincoln was, to Booth, a great tyrant, Seward was presumably a lesser tyrant, but a tyrant still. The secretary may have owed his notoriety, in Booth's eyes, in part to his role in suspending civil liberties in the North, but to a Negrophobe like Booth it was probably Seward's earlier antislavery rhetoric that made him a marked man. Access was facilitated by the fact that Seward's carriage accident had made him bedridden; Paine knew that his victim was upstairs in the Old Clubhouse. In all likelihood, it was only the brave Robinson who kept Seward from sharing Lincoln's fate.

Several years later, Leonard Swett, a longtime Lincoln associate, called on Seward at the State Department. After some general conversation, Swett asked tentatively whether the secretary would let him see the scars left by Paine's knife. Seward obligingly removed his cravat, unbuttoned his collar, and showed Swett by how narrow a margin Paine had missed the great artery. He then remarked sadly that Providence had done him a bad turn in not allowing him to die with Lincoln: "I think I deserved the reward of dying there."[14]

Seward might have spoken differently had he foreseen the key role that would fall to him in the forthcoming Alaska purchase.

CHAPTER 18

The Second Surrender

ON A SPRING DAY in 1865 an unscheduled train chuffed into the depot at Greensboro, North Carolina. The peaceful town of 2,000, all but ignored during four years of civil war, found itself a reluctant host to what remained of the government of the Confederacy. Aboard the train, which had left Danville, Virginia, 12 hours before, were President Jefferson Davis and most of his cabinet. A second train carried a considerable cargo of Confederate gold.

Richmond had fallen on April 3. With Confederate currency now all but worthless, ladies of the former capital were reduced to selling pastry to the Yankees in order to secure bread for their own tables. Six days later, on April 9, Robert E. Lee's Army of Northern Virginia had surrendered at Appomattox. Lee told a group of his solders, "I have done my best for you. My heart is too full to say more."

In the South as in the North, the fall of Richmond and the surrender by Lee were seen as signaling an end to a war that had killed more than 600,000 people and been responsible for total casualties of more than 1 million. Suggestions that the war might not be over were unpopular, and the reception accorded the Davis party at Greensboro was cool. One young Confederate soldier, eyeing the decrepit train that had brought Davis south from Richmond, characterized the president and his retinue as "a government on wheels . . . the marvelous and incongruous debris of the wreck of the Confederate capital."

Spring had come to North Carolina, but there was war-weariness everywhere. In Greensboro there was also fear—fear of the embittered parolees from Lee's army who were filtering into the town, and most of all, fear of Sherman. Sherman's Yankee army was approaching, and nothing the South could do seemed to slow his advance.

One person for whom the war was not over was Jefferson Davis. Four years of war had left the Confederate president pale and wan, afflicted with

The Confederacy's Last Days: Autumn 1864–Spring 1865

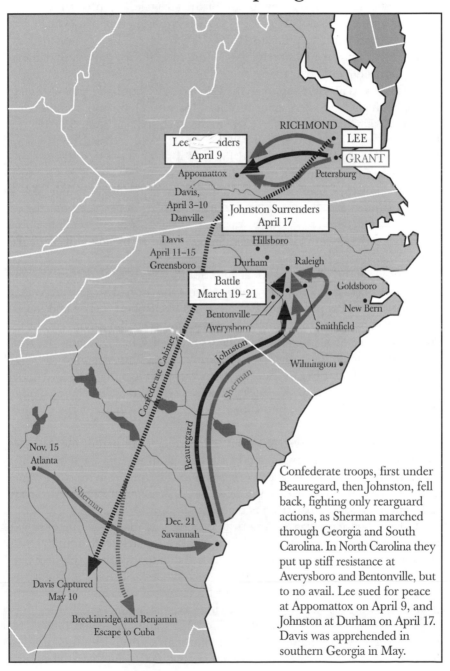

RICHMOND

LEE

Lee Surrenders
April 9

GRANT

Appomattox

Petersburg

Davis,
April 3–10
Danville

Johnston Surrenders
April 17

Davis
April 11–15
Greensboro

Hillsboro

Durham

Raleigh

Goldsboro

Battle
March 19–21

New Bern

Bentonville
Averysboro

Smithfield

Confederate Cabinet

Johnston

Wilmington

Sherman

Beauregard

Nov. 15
Atlanta

Sherman

Dec. 21
Savannah

Davis Captured
May 10

Breckinridge and Benjamin
Escape to Cuba

Confederate troops, first under Beauregard, then Johnston, fell back, fighting only rearguard actions, as Sherman marched through Georgia and South Carolina. In North Carolina they put up stiff resistance at Averysboro and Bentonville, but to no avail. Lee sued for peace at Appomattox on April 9, and Johnston at Durham on April 17. Davis was apprehended in southern Georgia in May.

insomnia and a variety of other ailments. But the 56-year-old Mississippian was no less convinced of the justice of this cause in 1865 than he had been four years earlier. From Danville he had issued yet another call to arms. "We have now entered upon a new phase of the struggle," he proclaimed. "Relieved from the necessity of guarding particular points, our army will be free to move from point to point to strike the enemy. . . . Let us not then despond, my countrymen; but relying on God, meet the foe with fresh defiance and . . . unconquerable hearts."

Defiance was in short supply in the Confederacy, but had Davis chosen to do so, he might have cited some numbers. Joseph E. Johnston, commanding the only Confederate force of any size in the East, still had some 30,000 men. Gen. Richard Taylor had perhaps 20,000 more. And across the Mississippi lay Davis's main hope, a scattered force of 40,000, mostly in Texas, commanded by Gen. Edmund Kirby Smith. Any wishful thinking based on these numbers, however, overlooked several pertinent facts. One was that Federal forces included a million men under arms with whom to confront the remaining Confederates. Another was that Sherman's army, totaling about 80,000 effectives, was close by, threatening to end all meaningful resistance east of the Mississippi.

No other name struck such fear into Southern hearts as that of William Tecumseh Sherman. The wiry red-bearded Ohioan had begun the war in obscurity. Whereas prominent Confederates like Robert E. Lee and Joseph E. Johnston had risen to senior ranks in the Old Army, Sherman was the ex-superintendent of a little-known military academy in Louisiana. In 1861 something resembling a nervous breakdown had almost ended his Civil War career before it began. But Sherman was then assigned to serve under Gen. Ulysses S. Grant in Kentucky. Teamed with Grant, he contributed to the series of Federal triumphs along the Mississippi that cut the Confederacy in two.

Sherman eventually was given an independent command, the Army of the Tennessee. After his augmented force had captured Atlanta in November 1864, he asked for and received permission to cut loose from his supply lines and "march to the sea." In devastating Georgia's economy en route to Savannah, Sherman set the pattern for total war.

"Cump" Sherman was an American original. He made a virtue of simple dress and simple life in the field. His men affectionately called him "Uncle Billy"; he in turn would sometimes stop and talk to groups of soldiers, bantering with them in his gruff, staccato manner. Like Davis, Sherman was something of an insomniac. He could be found in the small hours of the morning pacing his camp, poking a dying fire, visiting pickets.

Sherman hated war but liked soldiers and soldiering. Even though his brother John was a senator from Ohio, Sherman's greatest ire was reserved for politicians and newspaper reporters. He had no strong views on slavery, but had given a great deal of thought to how the war should be prosecuted. He saw the destruction of the Confederate economy as a means of hastening the end of the war, and he had no apology for the devastation his army wreaked. His march to the sea contributed only indirectly to the defeat of Lee's army, but it sapped the morale of the entire Confederacy.

Sherman had done little to control looting while his army was in South Carolina, for he shared his soldiers' animosity toward the state that had for so long been identified with secession. Discipline was tightened somewhat as the army crossed into North Carolina, and personal property was spared in some instances. Nonetheless, army foragers—or "bummers," as they were called—continued to roam the countryside in advance of the regular troops, "requisitioning" supplies. And entire pine forests, tapped for turpentine, were burned by soldiers for sport. The conflagrations were tremendous.

Sherman, at his headquarters near Smithfield, knew that organized Confederate resistance was near an end. But he was eager to see a formal surrender, lest Johnston's army disperse into guerrilla bands that might prolong the fighting indefinitely. In late March, Sherman had attended a conference aboard the gunboat *River Queen*—a meeting that had included President Abraham Lincoln, Grant, and Rear Adm. David Dixon Porter—at which Lincoln had stated his desire to get the Rebel armies "back to their homes, at work on their farms and in their shops." Sherman thought he knew the kind of peace the president had in mind. From Raleigh he wired Secretary of War Edwin Stanton, "I will accept the same terms as General Grant gave General Lee, and be careful not to complicate any points of civil policy."

Sherman's outnumbered opponent was the makeshift Confederate army of Gen. Joseph E. Johnston. Although Johnston had been unable to obstruct Sherman's march through the Carolinas, he had kept an army in the field and had fought tenacious delaying actions where circumstances permitted. On March 19 at Bentonville, North Carolina, he had thrown his little army against one wing of Sherman's command and had managed to come within an ace of victory.

Joe Johnston was one of the enigmas of the Civil War. The dapper, courtly Virginian made no attempt to mingle with his soldiers, as Sherman did, yet he was perhaps as respected by his men as Robert E. Lee had been by the Army of Northern Virginia. His superiors, however, had difficulties with Johnston. At the outset of the war Davis had named three other generals, Lee among them, senior to Johnston, despite the fact that Johnston had out-ranked them in the Old Army. Johnston protested the slight and never forgave Jefferson Davis.

It was Johnston who had confronted Sherman in the campaign for Atlanta, and although Johnston directed a skillful delaying action, Davis had relieved him in July 1864 for failing to halt the Yankee advance. When Johnston's successors had even worse luck against the rampaging Sherman, the wily Johnston, always formidable in defense, was restored to command. From the time of Lee's surrender, however, Johnston believed that his duty lay in making a decent peace.

At Greensboro, Davis was met by Gen. P.G.T. Beauregard, another senior officer with whom Davis had crossed swords. Beauregard, now second in command to Johnston, had opened the war with the capture of Fort Sumter and a subsequent victory at the First Battle of Manassas. Since then his reputation had been in eclipse. At Greensboro, however, Beauregard greeted Davis cordially. He advised Davis that Johnston would be arriving the following day, April 12, and moved his headquarters, located in a baggage car, to a railroad siding within sight of Davis's train.

At the cabinet meeting on April 12, Davis proposed re-forming the Army of Virginia, apparently ignoring the fact that the paroles granted to Lee's soldiers were conditioned on their not bearing arms against the Union. Johnston heard the president out in disdainful silence, and when he spoke it was in a tone of rebuke. In Johnston's view, the South now lacked both money and munitions, and to protract the war would be a crime. "The effect of our keeping [to] the field," he said, "would be, not to harm the enemy, but to complete the devastation of our country and the ruin of its people."

Johnston counterproposed that peace negotiations be initiated with Sherman at once. He was supported in this idea by all the cabinet members in attendance except for Secretary of State Judah P. Benjamin. But Johnston reckoned without Jefferson Davis. Writing his memoirs two decades later, Davis recalled, "I had reason to believe that the spirit of the army in North Carolina was unbroken, for, though surrounded by circumstances well calculated to depress and discourage them, I had learned that they earnestly protested to their officers against . . . surrender."

That afternoon the Confederate Secretary of War, John C. Breckinridge, arrived at Greensboro. Breckinridge had been vice president of the United States under James Buchanan, and an opponent of secession until nearly three months after First Manassas. He had served the Confederacy as a major general and enjoyed a wide measure of respect among Confederate leaders. After meeting with Johnston and Beauregard, Breckinridge agreed that further resistance was useless.

He joined Davis's cabinet meeting on April 13. Around a table in the drab railroad car, Davis once again expressed confidence in victory, and then asked Johnston for his views. Johnston reiterated his pessimistic assessment of the previous day–"My small force is melting away like snow before the sun"–and stated flatly that the South was tired of war. Of those present, only Benjamin again supported Davis in his view that the war should continue. Reluctantly, Davis authorized Johnston to open negotiations with Sherman. Johnston could offer to disband Confederate troops and to recognize Federal authority, but only on condition that state governments in the South would be preserved and that Southerners would not be penalized for their rebellion. The status of former slaves was not even mentioned.

While Davis and his colleagues drafted a letter for Johnston to send to Sherman, their world continued to collapse around them. Pillaging soldiers roamed the streets of Greensboro, undeterred by the presence of the Confederate cabinet and much of the army high command. Navy Captain John Taylor Wood, who was a member of Davis's party, wrote, "Troops greatly demoralized, breaking into and destroying the public stores."

Because Johnston's letter was delayed in reaching Sherman, who had just established headquarters at Raleigh, their first meeting was set for April 17, eight days after Lee's surrender. Sherman had boarded the train that would take him to the rendezvous when a telegrapher ran up to say that an important telegram, in cipher, had just arrived. Sherman delayed his departure, and 30 minutes later was reading a message from Stanton that told of the assassination of Lincoln and the assault on Secretary of State Seward. Swearing the telegrapher to secrecy, Sherman folded the telegram into his pocket and told the engineer to proceed.

At about 10 A.M. Sherman's train reached Durham, where a squadron of Union cavalry was waiting. Sherman and his entourage, under a white flag, rode for five miles along the Hillsboro road, where they met Johnston and his party. In Sherman's words:

> We shook hands, and introduced our respective attendants. I asked if there was a place convenient where we could be private, and General Johnston said he had passed a small farmhouse a short distance back. . . . We rode back to it together side by side, our staff officers and escorts following.

Sherman and Johnston had never met, but in the course of the previous months they had developed a healthy professional respect for one another. Alone in the parlor of a farmer named James Bennitt, Sherman passed Johnston the telegram from Stanton and watched his antagonist closely.

> The perspiration came out in large drops on his forehead, and he did not attempt to conceal his distress. He denounced the act as a disgrace to the age, and hoped I did not charge it to the Confederate Government. I told him I could not believe that he or General Lee, or the officers of the Confederate army, could possibly be privy to acts of assassination; but I would not say as much for Jeff. Davis.

The two soldiers quickly agreed that there should be no more fighting. But Sherman was bound by the terms that Grant had accorded Lee, and

Johnston in theory was bound by the instructions that Davis had given him. The Virginian, prompted by his contempt for Jefferson Davis, had an idea: Why not "make one job of it" and settle the fate of all Confederates still under arms? Sherman was tempted, but he was also realistic. Could Johnston in fact deliver "all armies to the Rio Grande?" Johnston pointed out that Secretary of War Breckinridge was close at hand, and that Breckinridge's orders would be obeyed anywhere. It was sunset when the two generals parted, to meet the following day.

Sherman's immediate task, on returning to his headquarters, was to break the news of Lincoln's assassination. He first ordered all soldiers to camp, then issued a bulletin announcing the death of the president but exonerating the Confederate army from complicity in the assassination. Sherman and his generals watched their men closely. Many wept, and some demanded a final battle to avenge Lincoln, but Sherman's handling of the announcement prevented any serious breakdown of discipline.

On the morning of April 18, Sherman set off to meet with Johnston again, determined, in Sherman's words, "to manifest real respect for [Lincoln's] memory by following, after his death that policy which, if living, I felt certain he would have approved." At the Bennitt farmhouse the two men resumed their talks. Johnson asked Sherman about the status of whites in the South. Were they "the slaves of the people of the North?" Nonsense, Sherman replied; Southerners would be "equal to us in all respects" once they had submitted to Federal authority. Johnston was leading his conqueror into uncharted waters, but Sherman seemed oblivious to the danger. When Johnston suggested that they bring Breckinridge into their talks, Sherman at first refused, but when Johnston pointed out that Breckinridge might participate in his capacity as a Confederate general, Sherman assented.

Johnston and Breckinridge attempted to outline terms for Davis's personal surrender, but Sherman refused to deal on the basis of individuals. Then a courier arrived with surrender terms drafted by the Confederate postmaster general, John Reagan, in Greensboro. Sherman looked them over, but set them aside as too general and too verbose. He took pen in hand himself and began to write. At one point he rose, walked to his saddlebag, took out a bottle, and poured himself a long drink of whiskey. After sipping his drink at the window, he returned to his drafting. Shortly thereafter he passed a paper to Johnston with the remark, "That's the best I can do."

Sherman's terms were sweeping. They called for all Confederate armies "now in existence" to be disbanded and all soldiers paroled. Existing state governments would continue, once their personnel had sworn allegiance to the Union. The inhabitants of all the Southern states were guaranteed their political rights, as defined by the Constitution. There was no mention of slavery or of the status of former slaves. Sherman's only hedge was in the final paragraph, where the signatories pledged "to obtain the necessary authority . . . to carry out the above program."

Sherman and Johnston signed the document and parted on warm terms. As Johnston and Breckinridge rode away, Johnston asked what Breckinridge thought of their antagonist. "Oh, he's bright enough and a man of force, but Sherman is a hog," the Kentuckian responded. "Did you see him take that drink by himself?" asked Breckinridge, who was himself well known for his hard drinking. Johnston replied that Sherman had only been absentminded, but Breckinridge was unforgiving. "No Kentucky gentleman would ever have taken that bottle away. He knew how much we needed it."

President Andrew Johnson was meeting with his cabinet when Grant, who was there by special invitation, outlined the terms agreed to by Sherman and Johnston. The cabinet was shocked: The terms went far beyond those of Appomattox and constituted a virtual peace treaty. Particularly galling was the section that recognized the legality of the state governments in the South. When it became clear that the administration would not accept Sherman's agreement, Grant offered to go in person to Sherman and explain why his terms had been disapproved. The new president agreed to this, telling Grant to order Sherman to annul the April 18 agreement and to draft new terms applicable only to Johnston's army.

Meanwhile, Sherman and Johnston awaited word from their respective superiors. Grant sent Sherman a telegram, then departed by oceangoing steamer to Beaufort, South Carolina. There he would have to find a train to take him north. He kept his mission a secret because he wanted to avoid publicly embarrassing Sherman. The Confederate cabinet agreed to Sherman's terms on April 23, after Attorney General George Davis had noted cheerfully, "Taken as a whole the convention amounts to this: that the states of the Confederacy shall reenter the old Union upon the same footing on which they stood before seceding from it."

Sherman received Grant's telegram that same day and took the rejection of his terms calmly. In the five days since the signing of the treaty, he may have come to regret its scope if not its spirit. Sherman wrote Stanton on April 25 that "I admit my folly in embracing in a military convention any civil matters," but added that he had understood from Stanton that "the financial state of the country demanded military success and would warrant a little bending [as] to policy. I still believe that the General Government of the United States has made a mistake, but that is none of my business."

Sherman called for a third meeting, and on April 26, 17 days after Appomattox, he met Johnston again at Bennitt's farm. Sherman explained the need for new terms of surrender, and he and Johnston quickly signed a five-point convention. It surrendered Johnston's army but took no account of other Confederate forces and avoided all political matters. As with Lee's army, officers and men were permitted to return to their homes. By establishing a rapport with Johnston, Sherman had effectively prevented any resort to guerrilla warfare on the part of Johnston's forces—the result that he had feared most.

Johnston, who may have anticipated a disavowal of Sherman's April 18 terms, issued a brief statement to his soldiers: Lee's surrender and the disintegration of the Confederacy's industrial base had destroyed all hope of successful war. He had therefore surrendered "to spare the blood of this gallant little army, [and] to prevent further sufferings."

So the war wound to a close. On May 4, at Mobile, Alabama, Confederate Gen. Richard Taylor surrendered his Alabama-Mississippi command in accordance with the terms granted Lee and Johnston. Three weeks later, on May 26, the Trans-Mississippi forces of Gen. E. Kirby Smith, the last Confederate army of any size, stacked their arms. President Davis and his entourage were captured in Georgia on May 10; the Confederate president would be incarcerated for two years before being released in 1867. Two important figures, however, broke off from the Davis group and set out on their own: Breckinridge and Benjamin eventually made it to Cuba. Breckinridge later returned with a presidential pardon; Benjamin lived out a prosperous life in England.

As the Confederacy collapsed, Sherman became further involved in the surrender imbroglio. The way in which the administration repudiated his original terms soured relations between Sherman and Stanton, the acerbic secretary of war. In the course of informing the press of the terms that Sherman had offered Johnston, Stanton suppressed a letter in which Grant had characterized Sherman as believing that he was acting in accordance with Lincoln's wishes. Rather, Stanton announced that Sherman had deliberately ignored Lincoln's instructions, as reiterated by President Johnson. Not content with these allegations of insubordination, Stanton charged Sherman with having made troop dispositions that would facilitate Davis's escape with his supposed hoard of Confederate gold, and virtually accused Sherman of disloyalty. The *New York Herald* declared that "Sherman's splendid military career is ended; he will retire under a cloud. . . . With a few unlucky strokes of his pen, he has blurred all the triumphs of his sword."

Sherman had not protested the overruling of his terms, but word of Stanton's charges infuriated him. He wrote to Grant, saying that he had never in his life disobeyed an order, "though many and many a time I have risked my life, health and reputation in obeying orders." Toward the end of May, Sherman appeared before the Committee on the Conduct of the War; he said that his April 18 terms, although not specifically authorized by Lincoln, would have been authorized by him had he lived.

In Washington, Sherman took his revenge in the most public way possible when the capital celebrated the end of the war with a two-day military review. Sherman's army paraded on the second day, May 24, and after passing President Johnson in the reviewing stand set up in front of the White House, Sherman dismounted and joined the reviewing party. He saluted the president and shook hands. But when Stanton, standing next to the president, started to extend his hand, Sherman, flushing deeply, ignored him; instead, the general shook hands with Grant and turned to watch the parade. Such was Sherman's prestige that his discourtesy went without rebuke.

Sherman never forgave Stanton. In contrast, the negotiations at Bennitt's farmhouse began a lasting friendship between Sherman and Johnston. Sherman went on to become commanding general of the army, while Johnston served a term in Congress and was later appointed commissioner of railroads by President Grover Cleveland. When Sherman died in 1891—reviled in the South but widely admired in the North—one of the honorary pallbearers was Joseph E. Johnston. The day of the funeral was cold and rainy, and Johnston was by then 82. "General, please put on your hat," a member of the party admonished. "You might get sick." Johnston replied, "If I were in his place, and he were standing here in mine, he would not put on his hat."

In 10 days, Johnston, too, was dead.

CHAPTER 19

■

Admiral on Horseback

ON JUNE 19, 1864, the U.S. steam sloop *Kearsarge* put an end to the fabled Confederate commerce destroyer *Alabama*, sending the her to the bottom of the English Channel in a battle that lasted slightly over one hour. Had the *Alabama*'s famous captain, Raphael Semmes, been made a prisoner on board the *Kearsarge*, he might well have faced trial as a pirate. Instead, he had the good fortune to be rescued by an English yacht, the *Deerhound*, which took him and several of his officers to Britain, where they were warmly received.

Even in defeat, Semmes's place in naval history was assured. Of the 200-odd Northern merchantmen destroyed during the war, Semmes—first in the *Sumter* and then in the famous *Alabama*—accounted for no fewer than 71. In defeating the Federal gunboat *Hatteras* off Galveston, Texas, in January 1863, he had become the only Confederate captain to sink an enemy warship in single combat.

Semmes, now 55 years old, had no prospect of another command, and no one would have criticized him had he chosen to wait out the war in England. But Semmes was a Southerner to the core, and he was determined to share in whatever the future held for the South. He would return to Richmond and serve however he could. After a six-week holiday on the Continent, Semmes and several others booked passage to Matamoros, Mexico, the only route home that did not require running through the Federal blockade. From Matamoros, Semmes crossed to Brownsville, Texas, where he wrote to a friend in England of his emotions on returning to the South for the first time in three years:

> Even the uninviting sand banks of the Texas coast looked pleasant, and I felt a strange thrill as I placed my foot again upon my native land; all the more dear to me for her agony of blood & misery. . . . I

fear the nation which awaits me, as I pass through this half-lawless, while chivalrous, warm-hearted state, even more than I do the four weeks journey by stage & on horseback, before me.[1]

The *Alabama* had made Semmes famous in the South. On November 13 he headed for Shreveport, with a coach and cavalry escort provided by the local Confederate commander. Remarkably, for a country in its fourth year of war, the coach was well stocked with brandy, which Semmes disdained, and Havana cigars, which he fully enjoyed. His journey across Texas became a triumphant procession. At towns like Houston, Hempstead, and Rusk, he was met by whooping Texans who often compelled him to make short speeches so that they might hear, in Semmes's ironic description, "how the pirate talked."[2]

While south Texas was relatively untouched by the war, the prospect changed as Semmes's party entered Louisiana. At Shreveport, Semmes met Gen. Edmund Kirby Smith, commanding the Trans-Mississippi Department, who told Semmes that his son Oliver was in Alexandria, 140 miles south, on the staff of Gen. Richard Taylor. Semmes now made a five-day trip to Alexandria, where Oliver was granted a leave of absence to accompany his father as far as Mobile, Alabama.

The two men, still with a small escort, left Alexandria on horseback on December 10, planning to link up with mail couriers to cross the Red River and the great Mississippi. Semmes and his son spent several days hiding in the swamps and bayous that fringed the rivers. Occasionally they had to cross a bayou, but it was the dry season, and the main obstacles were the thick undergrowth and branches that could knock a rider from the saddle. Joining some Confederate couriers at the town of Evergreen, the Semmeses reached the west bank of the Mississippi on the evening of December 13. Two Federal gunboats were anchored upstream, but they did not represent a serious barrier to crossing the river. Semmes released most of his escort and loaded supplies into a skiff provided by one of the couriers. The night was still, but the crossing was without incident. In Semmes's recollection, "As we shot within the shadows of the opposite bank, our conductor . . . gave a shrill whistle to ascertain whether all was right. The proper response came directly . . . and in a moment more we leaped on shore among friends."[3]

On December 15 Semmes reached Mobile, where he had a two-week reunion with his wife, Anne, whom he had not seen for more than three years. Then he left by train for Richmond, a journey that took no less than two weeks on the dilapidated Southern railways. Semmes thought the people of Georgia "terribly demoralized," but he could hardly have expected otherwise after Sherman's march.

In Richmond the erstwhile cruiser captain was accorded the honors that the South reserved for its heroes. Both houses of the Confederate congress adopted votes of thanks, and Semmes was invited to visit the floor. President Davis promoted him to admiral "for gallant and meritorious conduct in command of the steam-sloop *Alabama*." A few days later he was appointed commander of the James River squadron, the most prestigious naval command that the hard-pressed Confederacy could offer.

On February 18, 1865, Semmes hoisted his flag on one of the few remaining ironclads, the *Virginia*, on the James River a few miles south of Richmond. His command consisted of three ironclads, each mounting four guns, plus five wooden gunboats, none of which carried more than two guns. It was a sad little flotilla, but, assisted by powerful shore batteries, it effectively blocked any move against Richmond by water.

Semmes's immediate problem was to maintain some level of morale. Officers and men were crowded into close, uncomfortable quarters on vessels that Semmes compared to prison ships. Clothing was in short supply, and the men were often on half rations. The flotilla was manned by complements drawn largely from army units, and in assisting the navy, Lee's commanders did not send their best soldiers. Whereas Semmes's sailors on the *Sumter* and the *Alabama* had been competent sailors but not Southerners, he now commanded Southerners who were not competent seamen.

The admiral was sitting down to dinner at about 4:30 P.M. on April 2 when an aide announced the arrival of a dispatch from the Navy Department. Not anticipating anything of importance, Semmes finished his meal before reading the message. That Sunday dinner would be his last leisurely meal for some time, because the message from Secretary of the Navy Stephen Mallory informed Semmes that Lee was evacuating his lines and the government was leaving Richmond. Semmes was instructed to destroy his ships and to join Lee with the men of his small command.[4]

Semmes was annoyed that Lee had not communicated his intentions directly; much time could have been saved. The Alabamian did not know it, but Davis and his cabinet had already left Richmond by train. Semmes immediately called his captains to the *Virginia* and told them what lay ahead. When night fell he led his flotilla upstream toward Richmond. He was wondering how best to sink his ships without attracting attention when a series of explosions on the north side of the James, caused by Lee's commanders destroying their ordnance, made such caution unnecessary. Just below the capital Semmes evacuated his three ironclads and crowded their crews onto the gunboats. Then, making good use of the experience gained on the *Sumter* and the *Alabama*, he fired the ironclads. The *Virginia*, loaded with munitions, exploded with a pyrotechnic display that shook houses in Richmond.

With the morning light Semmes disembarked his command below the capital and burned his gunboats. His was now exclusively a land command, one that desertion had reduced to perhaps 450 men, and Semmes had no illusions about their effectiveness as a land force. They were carrying heavy loads that included bedding, clothing, and mess gear, as well as food, sugar, tea, and tobacco. Worse still, they were incapable of marching any distance without becoming footsore.

Although prospects for his command were not bright, Semmes was not about to admit defeat. Because his "troops" were incapable of sustained marching, he headed for the railroad depot. With the enemy at the gates, discipline was disintegrating in the capital. The city's military commander, Gen. Richard S. Ewell, had attempted to destroy a supply of whiskey in a warehouse, but his guards could not prevent a mob—largely civilian—from becoming drunk and ugly. Many of the rowdies now headed, like Semmes, for the railroad station, in the hope of finding a train headed south.[5]

When Semmes reached the station at the head of his motley column, he was told that the last train had left hours before. For perhaps the last time in the war the gray eyes flashed. Semmes did *not* believe that the last rolling stock was gone, and would see for himself! Working their way through the station, which had been largely abandoned by its staff, Semmes and his officers found "a few straggling railroad cars" filled with Richmond residents still hoping that there might be one more train out of the city. Semmes ordered the civilians out, telling those who complained that it was better for noncombatants than for armed soldiers to be taken by the enemy. The cars were then coupled and the James River sailors marched on board. Semmes told his navy engineers to see what they could do with a small steam engine that had been abandoned in the depot.[6]

By then it was nearly 8:30 A.M., and Federal troops were entering the city. In the station yard, Confederate marines knocked down a picket fence and fed the wood into the locomotive's engine. Coupled to the heavily loaded cars, the little engine inched its way out of the depot in a cloud of smoke and sparks. It soon reached a woodpile where the engineers were able to load better fuel, and Semmes now allowed civilians to fill such space as remained in the cars. The train moved out of the yards and across the James, but at a slight grade on the west side of the river the straining locomotive wheezed to a halt. From the stalled train Semmes could see the columns of blue infantry, within easy rifle range, marching into the abandoned capital.

Semmes was considering his options when one of his engineers discovered a second locomotive abandoned nearby. The navy men coupled it to the first engine, and by midmorning the train was moving westward at about six miles per hour. From time to time it stopped to pick up stragglers—many of them, according to Semmes, generals and colonels—from the stream of refugees headed west. The train passed through Amelia Courthouse at dusk, having traveled 30 miles since leaving Richmond.

Semmes had kept some form of journal throughout the war. Now, in the pandemonium that accompanied the collapse of the Confederacy, he chronicled the debacle in a diary. "Great consternation along the roads," he wrote on April 3.[7] The train passed through Burkeville Junction at about 2:00 A.M. on April 4, 90 minutes before the town was attacked by Sheridan's cavalry.

Semmes's orders had been to join Lee's retreating army, but at this point he and his sailors were prepared to go wherever their train would take them. All day on April 4 it moved through southern Virginia, reaching Danville, where Davis and his cabinet had established a "temporary capital," at nightfall. Semmes's navy brigade was the last force of any size to escape from Richmond. Indeed, Semmes's achievement in extricating his little command from the James may have been as remarkable as any of his earlier feats at sea.

The next morning Semmes had breakfast with President Davis, who congratulated him on his escape. The president had just issued another call to arms, proclaiming a new phase of the struggle, but the response, even among his own entourage, was cool. Nevertheless, Secretary of the Navy Mallory, in one of his last official acts, constituted Semmes's command as an army brigade. Davis, in turn, appointed Semmes a brigadier general, making him the only Confederate officer to hold flag rank in two services. The Alabamian thought that his navy rank entitled him to be a major general, but he recognized that it was folly to debate the matter under the circumstances.[8]

When Semmes reviewed his command he found that he still had about 400 men. These he divided into two skeleton regiments, each commanded by one of his ship captains. After some rudimentary artillery drill, "General" Semmes deployed his command to defend the two bridges that spanned the Dan River. He and part of his command remained outside the town for 10 days, but not all of his men could be employed in the fortifications; those not in the trenches fished in the river or gathered to write letters home. The first news of Lee's surrender on April 9 came from paroled soldiers of the Army of Northern Virginia who streamed into Danville. Semmes was touched by the sight of these men, "some on foot, some on horseback, some nearly famished . . . and others barely able to totter along from disease."[9]

To link up with Johnston's army, Davis and his cabinet traveled by rail to Greensboro, North Carolina, on the evening of April 10. Semmes and his command followed on foot five days later, but the movement turned into a disaster. The march south, much of it in heavy rain, proved an invitation to fresh desertions. The following day brought the possibility of action against the enemy, as Semmes received an order from Gen. P.G.T. Beauregard to take his brigade to a break in the railroad outside Greensboro and protect supplies there. This required a countermarch of more than seven miles by footsore sailors and prompted new desertions. Semmes, who was sick, wrote in his journal that evening, "A stream of vagabonds passing—some Lee's men—many [others are] deserters who are seizing horses & otherwise robbing & plundering as they go."[10]

While Semmes and his command slogged their way south, Davis was meeting with his cabinet in Greensboro. At first Davis insisted on continuing the war. He proposed re-forming the Army of Northern Virginia, seemingly oblivious to the fact that the paroles granted to Lee's soldiers were conditioned on their not bearing arms against the Union. When a poll of the cabinet revealed only one vote—that of Secretary of State Judah P. Benjamin—for continuing the struggle, Davis reluctantly authorized Johnston to request surrender terms from Sherman.

Semmes and his bedraggled little band reached Greensboro on April 18. By this time his "brigade" had dwindled to perhaps 150 men. Even as Semmes set up camp, Johnston and Sherman were agreeing on terms of surrender—terms so sweeping and generous that they were subsequently repudiated in Washington. Semmes, however, was not interested in the terms. On arriving in Greensboro he requested authorization from Johnston's deputy, Beauregard, to lead his command to the Trans-Mississippi Department and continue the fight. Beauregard replied that any officers who wished to depart could do so, but their units were to stay in place. Ultimately, Semmes, too, stayed in Greensboro.[11]

When the Sherman-Johnston agreement of April 18 was rejected in Washington, the two generals met again on April 26. They quickly agreed on a five-point convention that surrendered Johnston's army but took no account of any other Confederate forces and avoided political issues. As with Lee's army, officers and men were permitted to return to their homes.

But what about "pirates?" Semmes knew that he was hardly the typical Confederate officer, and decided to make some special arrangements. On April 30 he went to Johnston's headquarters, where he met with Johnston, Beauregard, and others, and asked that he and his officers be the first to meet with Federal parole commissioners. The next day Semmes and his staff rode into Greensboro, where Federal commissioners had set up an office in the Britannia Hotel. After being introduced to Gen. George L. Hartsuff, the senior Federal commissioner, Semmes produced the muster roll for his command, and Hartsuff gave him presigned parole certificates for the number of names that appeared on it. This was not good enough for Semmes, who asked that his own form be filled out and witnessed in Hartsuff's presence. The Federals were puzzled but offered no objection. Semmes signed himself "Rear-Admiral in the Confederate States Navy and Brigadier-General in the Confederate States Army, commanding a brigade." When he walked out of the hotel, he carried with him a promise that he was not to be disturbed by Federal authorities so long as he obeyed the laws of the United States. Semmes was a survivor. He had survived the sinking of the *Alabama* and he fully intended to survive the wreck of the Confederacy.

Semmes returned to his camp outside Greensboro and distributed paroles to those of his command who remained. If he had any parting words, no

Thomas Nast's
portrayal of
"Semmes the
pirate." *U.S. Army
Military History
Institute*

record of them has survived. That same day he set out on the long journey home, some 900 miles through the devastated South. His route would be by road to Montgomery, Alabama, from where he hoped to take a boat to Mobile. With him were his youngest son, Raphael, who had been a midshipman during the war, three unidentified "servants," and several officers, including one veteran of the *Alabama*, Lt. Joe Wilson. Between them they had a single wagon and several mules, but not enough for all to ride.

The parolees covered 11 miles the first afternoon, camping at Jamestown on the road to Salisbury. Semmes wrote in his diary, "Highway filled with soldiers singly & in small parties, many leading half-starved horses & all ragged and dirty."[12] The roads were bad and forage was scarce. In addition, the travelers were bedeviled by a balky wagon wheel that required repeated repairs. The weather was fine, however, and Semmes and his entourage could generally cover between 20 and 28 miles per day. On May 6, while Joe Wilson went into a town to see about repairs to the wagon, Semmes bathed in a mountain stream. Two days later the wagon wheel expired once and for all near the South Carolina border. Perhaps because of these logistical problems, Semmes had unkind words for the residents of Spartanburg County, South Carolina. "Population ignorant, idle, thriftless; women young & old slovenly and dirty," he wrote.[13]

The navy party carried some provisions, which they supplemented with fruit and dairy products as best they could. How they paid local farmers, if they paid at all, is not recorded. At Greenville, South Carolina, which Semmes thought "a pretty village," the town council provided them with four days' rations. When they crossed into Georgia, Semmes was surprised to find many plantations still operating with black labor. Occasionally, Federal soldiers stopped the travelers, but they were allowed to proceed on showing their paroles.

On May 21, at the Alabama border, Semmes bade farewell to Joe Wilson, who left to go to his home in Florida. On May 22 the remainder of the Semmes party crossed the Chattahoochee River into Alabama, arriving at Montgomery on May 25. In 25 days since leaving Greensboro, the admiral and his party had traveled some 600 miles. From Montgomery, the travelers went their own ways. Semmes and young Raphael took passage on the river steamer *Peerless*, arriving in Mobile on about May 29.

The war was not quite over for Raphael Semmes. Before he had entirely settled down to a peacetime regimen, Semmes became one of the few Confederate officers whose wartime activities were so controversial that the terms of their parole were ignored. On December 15, 1865, he was arrested at his home outside Mobile and taken to Washington, where he was jailed for two months while the Andrew Johnson administration considered whether to try him for his "piratical" destruction of merchant vessels during the war. In the end, Semmes was quietly released, the government having reluctantly concluded that he had acted in accordance with the rules of war. Semmes returned to Mobile, characterizing his incarceration as "a flagrant violation of faith" by the United States.[14]

No category of Confederate veterans had a more difficult time after the war than navy men. Many knew only one form of life, that of the sea, and had given up any hope of advancement in the U.S. Navy when they sided with the Confederacy. Although Semmes had suffered financially as a result of the war, he had been a practicing lawyer at various times and now had his legal training to fall back on. It stood him in good stead, and for the rest of his life he earned a modest livelihood as an attorney in Mobile. In 1869 he published his *Memoirs of Service Afloat During the War Between the States*, the first important memoir by a senior Confederate, in which he revealed his continued bitterness over the war and its outcome. He died in 1877, the only Confederate officer able to sign himself "Rear Admiral, C.S.N., and Brig. General, C.S.A."

CHAPTER 20

———

"My God, You Cannot . . . Iron Me!

F OR SEVERAL WEEKS, the refugee column had slowly disintegrated. There was no panic, but the Confederacy had for all practical purposes come to an end with the surrender of Lee's army a month before. The remnants of the Confederate government straggled south, with little of the sense of mission that had sustained them for four years.

Near the town of Washington, Georgia, all soldiers who desired formal discharges were granted them and allowed to return home. The remaining wagons pressed on. Postmaster General John Reagan continued to process Post Office business. Others divided up such funds as remained. Despite rumors that Jefferson Davis had left Richmond with a great horde of Rebel gold, there wasn't a great deal left.

On the evening of May 9, 1865, the refugee column led by the president of the Confederate States of America was camped near the Oconee River, some 50 miles from the Florida border. Even after Appomattox, Davis still clung to hopes of linking up with surviving Confederate forces in Alabama and Mississippi and continuing the fight. But the war was over for Jefferson Davis. That night, the fugitives heard the sound of firing nearby. Grabbing one of his wife's shawls, the still-defiant Davis made for his horse. He had gone but a short distance when he was challenged by a Federal soldier and arrested.

In some countries Davis would not have survived the night of his capture. He had led an insurrection that had cost the lives of more than 600,000 people and devastated much of the land. At the close of the war, sentiment in the North had been inflamed by the assassination of Lincoln and the confirmation of primitive, if not brutal, conditions in Southern prisons. Although the soldiers of Lee's army had been paroled by Grant, Jeff Davis fell into a different category. For years Northern soldiers had gone to war singing, "We Will Hang Jeff Davis to a Sour Apple Tree." Now they had their man.

150

Davis's captors behaved very properly. The fugitives were first taken to Macon, Georgia—a four-day journey—but Davis and his wife, Varina, traveled in the relative comfort of a horse-drawn ambulance. The Davises were then lodged in the best hotel in Macon, while their captors speculated on whether they would be permitted to collect the $100,000 reward the Federal government had offered for Davis's capture.

In a few days, the more prominent prisoners were transferred by rail to Port Royal and put aboard a coastal steamer, the *William P. Clyde*. By then the prisoners included, in addition to Davis, Vice President Alexander H. Stephens, Sen. Clement Clay, and the famous cavalry commander Gen. Joe Wheeler. On May 19 the *Clyde* anchored off Hampton Roads. Advised that he was about to be separated from the other prisoners, Davis must have suspected that Fort Monroe, a massive bastion on the tip of Old Point Comfort, was to be his prison.

If there was ever an antithesis to the patrician Davis, it may have been the new commandant of Fort Monroe, Nelson A. Miles. The son of a Massachusetts farmer, Miles was clerking in a Boston store when the Civil War broke out. The youthful Miles recruited a company of Massachusetts militia and embarked on a career that would see him become the commanding general of the United States Army. In later years, Miles would become a bit of a caricature—a gouty old warrior with dreams of the presidency. But the dapper, ambitious Miles of 1865 was one of the army's authentic heroes. He had fought bravely at Harper's Ferry, Fredericksburg, and the Wilderness. Wounded four times, he was, at age 26, one of the youngest major generals in the army.

No jailor could expect an easy time with Jefferson Davis. The Confederate leader was rigid, convinced of his own rectitude, and brave. He was also hypersensitive to slights, and so aloof as to impress strangers as being cold and remote. The South's defeat on the battlefield had in no way led Davis to question the wisdom of his actions or the justice of his cause. He could not grasp the fact that the North viewed him as an archtraitor, one perhaps implicated in the assassination of Lincoln.

At Fort Monroe, Davis bade farewell to his wife, who would first take up residence in Savannah, Georgia. To Varina, Davis remained the god-husband whom she had venerated for 20 years:

> As the tug bore him away from the ship, he stood with bared head between the file of undersized [German-American] and other foreign soldiers . . . and as we looked, as we thought, our last upon his stately form and knightly bearing, he seemed a man of another and higher race.

Sketch by an unknown artist of Jefferson Davis in his first, damp cell at Fort Monroe, Virginia. *Library of Congress*

In the presence of Miles and Assistant Secretary of War Charles Dana, Davis was marched through the fort to the freshly whitewashed Casemate No. 2. Dana observed that the prisoner "bore himself with a haughty attitude. His face was somewhat flushed, but his features were composed and [his] step firm."

The Yankees took no chances with their famous prisoner. Not only did they install new bars in his cell, but they stationed two guards inside—perhaps to forestall any suicide attempt. In addition, Dana authorized Miles to manacle either Davis or Clement Clay whenever he thought such action necessary to make their imprisonment more secure.

Dana's order was discretionary, but he may have indicated to Miles that Davis's comfort was not of the utmost concern to the authorities in Washington. In any case, on the morning of May 23, Miles informed Capt. Jerome Titlow that he had decided to place Davis in ankle irons. He, Miles, would be away that afternoon; Titlow was to attend to the matter.

Just before sundown, Titlow, accompanied by a blacksmith and a blacksmith's helper, entered Davis's cell. Titlow advised the prisoner that he had "an unpleasant duty to perform," to which Davis, spying the blacksmith, exclaimed, "My God, you cannot have been sent to iron me!" Titlow responded that he had been so ordered, and asked for the prisoner's cooperation. Davis replied that he would never submit. The confrontation continued, with Titlow hoping to avoid force. Davis knew, Titlow said, that, as a soldier, he must execute an order. Titlow may have thought that he had carried his point, for at one point he motioned to the blacksmith to get to work. But by then Davis was furious; he shoved the blacksmith and began struggling with one of the guards. Titlow then brought in four soldiers to subdue his 57-year-old prisoner, and the blacksmith proceeded with his work.

Davis's unsuccessful resistance to his fetters offered an obvious parallel to the defeated South and provoked mixed reactions. In the South there was a surge of sympathy for Davis, who as president had never been an especially appealing figure. In the North, some newspapers applauded Miles's action, while others considered it unnecessary vengeance. The *London Times* editorialized against the harassment of a man "whom a little success would have transformed from a traitor to a monarch. The stake has been played fairly, and lost entirely, and the victor should be content with success."

Davis's cell, Fort Monroe, as seen in 1997.
Author's photo

The casemate at Fort Monroe in which Davis was imprisoned. *Author's photo*

Davis, the one-time slaveholder, would never forget the indignity of being placed in irons. Unknown to the prisoner, however, his prospects were looking up. His first benefactor was the prison physician, Col. John Craven. The doctor had no special affection for Davis, but on examining his patient he found Davis to be in poor health and no threat at all as a potential escapee. He recommended to Miles that Davis be put on a lighter diet than the standard prison fare and that the ankle irons be removed. Miles approved both recommendations, and five days after Davis had been manacled the fetters were removed.

The doctor-patient relationship blossomed into friendship. Eager for companionship and not permitted to converse with his guards, Davis came to look forward to his visits from the Yankee physician. Ruminating about the war, he spoke of Lincoln with respect and of Robert E. Lee and Stonewall Jackson with admiration bordering on awe. He was apprehensive about prospects for the freed slaves; nothing could persuade him that they had not been best off under a system of slavery that he saw a largely benevolent. Davis held strong views on other subjects as well, as suggested by this homily on womanhood as paraphrased by Craven:

> Woman's appearance in the political arena was a deplorable de-
> parture from the golden path which nature had marked out for

her. The male animal was endowed with far more than sufficient belligerency for all purposes of healthy agitation; and woman's part in the social economy, as she had been made beautiful and gentle, should be to soothe asperities rather than deepen and make more rough the crosstracks plowed in the road of life by the diverging passions and opinions of men.

Grudgingly, Davis fell in with the prison routine, which was not without its peculiarities. Because the authorities were still concerned lest Davis attempt suicide, he was not permitted a knife or fork; his food was cut in the prison kitchen. The turnover in spoons was considerable, for souvenir-hungry guards kept making off with their prisoner's one eating implement. Davis was permitted his pipe and tobacco, but his reading matter was limited to the Bible and the Episcopal prayerbook. For a time he was permitted no mail, and the only word of his family came from letters that Varina wrote Dr. Craven. For the first two months the prisoner was permitted no exercise, but from then on, thanks to Craven, he was allowed an hour's walk on the ramparts each day. And like many another political prisoner, Davis had a pet. When Craven once brushed aside some crumbs on Davis's cot, the prisoner complained that he had scattered the meal of his sole companion, a mouse.

Meanwhile, Craven continued to be concerned about his patient's health. Davis had a history of physical ailments; he had lost one eye to neuralgia, and suffered recurring bouts of malaria. Although Davis was something of a hypochondriac as well, Craven believed that his patient was badly debilitated and that his strength was being eroded by a persistent fever. One reason for the prisoner's low resistance was his difficulty in sleeping. Davis was an insomniac, and his problem was aggravated by the requirement that his cell be lighted at all times. Craven succeeded in having the lamp removed, but there was no improvement in what Craven called his patient's "general prostration." On September 2 he reported to Miles that Davis had become "despondent and dull, a very unnatural condition for him. He is evidently breaking down."

By this time both Miles and the War Department were aware that it would be impolitic for anything drastic to happen to Davis while he was in their custody. Hence, when Craven went on to suggest that some of his patient's problems might stem from the dampness of his cell, Miles approved his transfer to a lighter, airier room. No longer was Davis viewed as a potential escapee, and in his new surroundings he began a slow convalescence.

As 1865 turned to 1866, the omens for the prisoner were mixed. On the debit side, he was obliged to bid farewell to Dr. Craven, who was reassigned after a public furor over his having obtained a heavy overcoat for Davis, one that Northern papers pictured as fit for an emperor. (As a token of their friendship, Davis presented the doctor with one of the few gifts at his disposal, a prized meerschaum pipe.) Then, in April, the only other Confederate VIP still at Fort Monroe, Clement Clay, was quietly released. President Andrew Johnson, who had never cared for the patrician Davis, was proving more willing to pardon lesser Confederates than to alleviate the plight of their leader.

Nevertheless, help was in the offing. Varina Davis—no longer confined to Savannah—devoted herself to organizing a coalition of civil libertarians and friends of the Davis family to work for her husband's release. In July 1866, Horace Greeley, the eccentric but influential publisher of the *New York Tribune*, urged in an editorial that Davis be granted an early trial. Other Northerners indicated sympathy, and former president Franklin Pierce told Varina confidently that her husband would never be brought to trial. Two months later Dr. Craven published a short book, *The Prison Life of Jefferson Davis*, which portrayed the vanquished leader sympathetically, complete with pet mouse.

If Davis had problems, so did the U.S. government. A year had passed since Davis's arrest, and there was no credible evidence linking the Confederate government with the assassination of Lincoln. Although many Northerners would have delighted in trying Davis for treason, any such action would have major ramifications. If Davis were tried, how about members of his cabinet? How about Lee, who had been paroled, and the governors of the Confederate "states?" While Davis languished in Fort Monroe, the Johnson administration engaged special counsel to decide what to do with him. Johnson and his advisers may well have recalled Lincoln's expressed hope that Davis might escape the country and make these questions moot.

In the progressive relaxation of Davis's prison regimen, Varina was permitted to join him in May and to set up housekeeping in something resembling an efficiency apartment. At the same time, Davis's formal indictment on charges of treason—a seeming setback—proved to be the first in a series of maneuvers that would lead to freedom.

In December 1866 the Supreme Court ruled, in the case of *Ex Parte Milligan*, that civilians could not be tried by military tribunals in peacetime if civil courts were available. The decision was a break for Davis, for it effectively ruled out trial by a military tribunal such as that which had tried the Lincoln conspirators. As for a civil trial, no one could really imagine a Southern jury convicting Davis of treason, while an acquittal might even be interpreted as vindication of secession. The Johnson administration had no good options.

In the spring of 1867, Horace Greeley, accompanied by the reformer Gerrit Smith, made a pilgrimage to Richmond. There, on May 13, they signed a bail bond for $100,000, which meant freedom for Jefferson Davis almost exactly two years after his incarceration in Fort Monroe. A *New York World* correspondent wrote that after Greeley had signed, Davis stepped forward to shake his hand. According to the reporter, spectators laughed at the expression on Greeley's face, "so obvious was his pleasure."

And what of General Miles? Federal authorities had belatedly come to recognize that in Jefferson Davis they had a potential martyr on their hands. As a result, when Varina Davis made Miles the scapegoat for her husband's problems, Washington listened. Varina pulled no punches. Miles, she wrote, was "a beast, a hyena, and only 25 [*sic*] years old." On another occasion she referred to the commandant as "a boor, a plebe." The fury of her indignation seemed to go beyond Miles's brief, if overzealous, manacling of her husband. One suspects that, to the tart-tongued Varina, Miles's crowning defect was the he was from the wrong side of the tracks. In any case, Miles was reassigned in September 1866 and went on to new glory in the Indian wars.

Jefferson Davis, for all his fragile health, survived his release from prison by some 22 years, living until 1889. The charges against him were quietly dropped. Varina Davis lived well into the 20th century, ever zealous of her husband's reputation. When Miles became commanding general of the Army in 1895, Varina remained unimpressed. For Miles to have risen "from the depths of ignorance and brutality in which he lived" when she knew him, demonstrated only that he was "adroit, ambitious, unscrupulous and persistent."

In 1905 Miles published an article in which he defended his actions toward Davis, pointing out that at the time of the infamous manacling no one knew what Davis's role in the Lincoln assassination might have been. Varina was seriously ill at the time Miles's article appeared, but not too ill to commission a friend to write a rebuttal. She had it read and reread to her during her illness. According to the approving Varina, it was "a model denunciation of a vulgarian."

CHAPTER 21

Grover Cleveland and the Rebel Banners

GROVER CLEVELAND, the first Democrat to occupy the White House after the Civil War, brought important assets to his high post. He was hard-working, stubbornly honest, and independent-minded. He may not have been the first statesman to assert that "a public office is a public trust," but the statement so epitomized Cleveland that it is usually credited to him.

But the New Yorker also exhibited certain weaknesses, one of which was a remarkable insensitivity to some important political constituencies. When Jacob Coxey led an army of unemployed to protest in Washington, an unsympathetic Cleveland had Coxey arrested for trespassing on the Capitol grounds. Nor was Cleveland on the cutting edge of the movement for women's suffrage. "Sensible and responsible women do not want to vote," pronounced Cleveland. "The relative positions to be assumed by man and woman in the working out of our civilization were assigned long ago by an intelligence higher than ours."

As for the Civil War, Cleveland's great desire was to preside over a country that was reunited spiritually as well as politically. He appointed two Southerners to his cabinet, giving the South more than token representation for the first time since the war. He endorsed the unveiling of a statue of Confederate Gen. Albert Sidney Johnston, writing that every American could take pride in Johnston's nobility of character. He reveled in the warm welcome accorded him during a tour of the South in 1886.

The following summer he listened sympathetically when Secretary of War William Endicott suggested that it might be a graceful gesture to return to the erstwhile Confederate states the battle flags that had been captured from Southern forces during the Civil War, flags that were now moldering in the attic of the War Department. After all, the war had been over for more than two decades.

President Grover Cleveland's decision to return captured Confederate battle flags in 1887 may have cost him reelection. *Author's Collection*

Cleveland concurred, and the secretary of war moved on to the next item on his agenda. In agreeing to return the Rebel banners, however, Cleveland unwittingly precipitated a rhetorical tempest that would revive wartime passions and damage him politically.

Notwithstanding the passage of time, the Civil War remained vivid in the national memory. Union and Confederate veterans alike looked back with pride on their wartime exploits—and those of their comrades. Much of a soldier's pride was invested in his regiment. A unit's flag was to be defended to the death, and flags belonging to the enemy, many of which had been seized in hand-to-hand combat, were the most cherished of battlefield memorabilia.

Cleveland's decision revealed his imperfect understanding of the martial pride of Civil War veterans. He was the first president since the war not to have served in the Union army, and military service was a politically sore subject for him. As a young man, he and his two brothers had drawn straws to decide which of them would stay home and support their widowed mother. Grover had drawn the short straw and as a result had spent the war as a lawyer in Buffalo, New York. He hired a substitute, probably for $300, to go to war on his behalf.

Cleveland's noncombatant status did not endear him to those who had fought for the North, nor was this the only issue that made him suspect to the nation's most important veterans' organization, the Grand Army of the Republic (GAR). Even more infuriating was Cleveland's preoccupation with frugality in government. The president vetoed hundreds of private bills designed to place on the pension rolls veterans whose disabilities were unrelated to military service. Cleveland's repeated veto of pension bills brought forth a clamor from veterans, but the vetoes continued.

Then came the matter of the Rebel banners. After his meeting with the president in June 1887, Secretary Endicott sent circular letters to the Southern governors, advising them of Washington's plan to return the flags. When the news became public, however, there was a storm of Northern disapproval. The *New York Tribune* denounced the plan, calling the flags "mementos of as foul a crime as any in human history." Sen. Joseph Hawley of Connecticut, himself a veteran, wrote Cleveland that he was saddened by the president's action—that the best way to deal with flags taken from "our misguided brothers and wicked conspirators" was to burn them.

The first Northern governor to raise the alarm was Joseph B. Foraker of Ohio, who faced a tough campaign for reelection. "No rebel flags will be surrendered while I am governor," telegraphed "Fire Engine Joe," ignoring the fact that Cleveland's order applied only to those flags gathering dust in Washington. Foraker was quickly joined by a formidable ally, the commander in chief of the GAR, Gen. Lucius Fairchild. Speaking of Cleveland's order before a gathering of veterans, Fairchild thundered, "May God palsy the hand that wrote that order. May God palsy the brain that conceived it, and may God palsy the tongue that dictated it." Fairchild, who had lost an arm at the Battle of Gettysburg, was sometimes referred to romantically as "The Empty Sleeve." Soon the press was citing him as "the Fairchild of the three palsies."

As letters and telegrams—most of them critical—poured into the normally somnolent White House, Cleveland realized he had stirred up a hornet's nest. The New Yorker was a courageous man but he was not eager to take on the GAR. In a letter to Secretary Endicott on June 15, Cleveland advised that he had reconsidered the matter of the flags and had decided that their return by presidential edict "is not authorized by existing law nor justified as an Executive act." Disposition of the flags, he wrote, should be left to Congress.

If Cleveland thought this strategic retreat would bring the matter to a close, he was mistaken. The GAR, which numbered some 400,000 Union veterans, was the most formidable lobby in the country. Democrats and Republicans alike wooed the old soldiers with promises of pensions and other benefits, but in practice the organization was an offshoot of the Republican Party. It was the Republicans, "the party of Lincoln," for whom the veterans turned out on election day. Now, with a president in office who was perceived as antiveteran, the GAR was not prepared to let the flag issue die.

Cleveland had earlier accepted an invitation to visit the GAR at its annual encampment at St. Louis. After some strong hints from the GAR leadership, however, the president withdrew his acceptance. At a veterans' reunion in Wheeling, West Virginia, there was a near riot when some of the parading units refused to march under a banner that read, "God Bless Our President, Commander-in-Chief of Our Army and Navy."

Clearly the president had presented his political opponents with an emotional issue. Not everyone in the North, however, was impressed by the willingness of the GAR to revive sectional issues. A respected journal, the *Nation*, ridiculed Fairchild for his three palsies, and asked whether enough killing had not taken place in the war itself to satisfy even the GAR.

Nevertheless, Ohio's Foraker made political capital out of the flag blunder in his 1887 reelection bid. He campaigned that fall on the issue of Cleveland's "insults" to the country's "brave, battle-scarred veterans," insults that, in the view of some veterans, included Cleveland's having gone fishing on Memorial Day. Foraker's easy reelection signaled that the White House had suffered damage over the flag and pension episodes.

According to one study, the battle flag incident took up more newspaper space than any other issue during the summer of 1887. When Cleveland ran for reelection in 1888, he was defeated by Benjamin Harrison, a decorated veteran and staunch supporter of the GAR. To be sure, Harrison's victory was due to a quirk in the electoral college, for Cleveland, with all his problems, won 100,000 more popular votes than his opponent. But political observers agreed that the veterans' vote—crucial in states like Indiana and New York—had gone heavily against Cleveland.

The passions of any war die hard, and those aroused by a civil war take a particularly long time to heal. As the years went on, however, there was less refighting of the Civil War. Time took its toll on the ranks of the Grand Army of the Republic, and the Spanish-American War saw Northerners and Southerners once again fighting under the same flag.

By 1905, four decades after the war, there was a Republican in the White House, one still savoring his landslide reelection. Theodore Roosevelt, acting in close consultation with Congress, set about accomplishing the task that Cleveland had been unable to bring off. It was relatively easy. In February 1905 a bill to return Confederate battle flags passed both houses and was signed into law. It passed unanimously despite the fact that one of the senators was none other than "Fire Engine Joe" Foraker.

Acknowledgments and Notes

The author wishes to thank the following publications for permission to include articles that originally appeared in their pages:

American History Illustrated

Army

Civil War Times Illustrated

Military History Quarterly (MHQ)

Yankee

CHAPTER 1. "Compassion Is Always Due to An Enraged Imbecile"
First published in *American History Illustrated*, February 1976, and used by permission.

CHAPTER 2. "I Could Have Surrendered Washington"
First published in *Army* magazine, January 1979. Copyright 1979 by the Association of the U.S. Army and used by permission.

CHAPTER 3. Willard's of Washington
Adapted from an article in *American History Illustrated*, October 1979, and used by permission.

CHAPTER 4. Lieutenant Grant and the Missing Money
Adapted from an article in *Army* magazine, February 1982. Copyright 1982 by the Association of the U.S. Army and used by permission.

CHAPTER 5. Lincoln and Seward: A Washington Friendship
1. Glyndon G. Van Deusen, *William Henry Seward* (New York: Oxford University Press, 1967), 113.
2. Quoted in Gamaliel Bradford, *Union Portraits* (Boston: Houghton Mifflin, 1916), 207.
3. John M. Taylor, *William Henry Seward* (New York: HarperCollins, 1991), 2.
4. Carl Sandburg, *Abraham Lincoln: The War Years* (New York: Charles Scribner's, 1939), I, 145.
5. Van Deusen, *Seward*, 251.
6. Sandburg, *Abraham Lincoln: The War Years*, I, 180–81.

7. Bradford, *Union Portraits*, 212.
8. Frederick W. Seward, *Seward At Washington* (New York: Derby and Miller, 1891), 575.
9. Sandburg, *Abraham Lincoln: The War Years*, I, 184–85.
10. Van Deusen, *Seward*, 336.
11. Taylor, *William Henry Seward*, 208.
12. Ibid., 214.
13. Benjamin Thomas, *Abraham Lincoln* (New York: Alfred A. Knopf, 1952), 351.
14. Staudenraus, *Mr. Lincoln's Washington*, 61–62.
15. Gideon Welles, *Lincoln and Seward* (New York: Sheldon and Co., 1874), 43.
16. Taylor, *William Henry Seward*, 305.

CHAPTER 6. "You Are the Enemy of Our Set"
Adapted from an article first published in *Civil War Times Illustrated*, June 1979, and used by permission.

CHAPTER 7. The Bizarre Court-Martial of Thomas Knox
First published in *Yankee* magazine, January 1979, and used by permission.

CHAPTER 8. Farewell to the *Monitor*
1. Ruth White, *Yankee From Sweden*, 206.
2. *New York World*, Jan. 31, 1862.
3. Virgil C. Jones, *The Civil War at Sea*, (New York: Holt, Rinehart and Winston, 1960–62) II, 306.
4. A.A. Hoehling, *Thunder At Hampton Roads* (Englewood Cliffs, N.J.: Prentice-Hall Inc., 1976), 188.
5. Robert W. Daly, ed., *Aboard the USS Monitor: 1862*, 254.
6. Jones, *The Civil War at Sea*, II, 313.
7. Daly, *Aboard the USS Monitor: 1862*, 258.
8. *Official Records (Navy) (ORN)* Series 1, Vol. VIII, 348.

CHAPTER 9. "With More Sorrow Than I Can Tell"
Adapted from an article first published in *Civil War Times Illustrated*, April 1981, and used by permission.
1. Ibid., 80–81.
2. John M. Taylor, *Garfield of Ohio* (New York: W.W. Norton, 1970), 86–87.

CHAPTER 10. The Night War Came to Portland, Maine
1. Jim Dan Hill, *Sea Devils of the Sixties* (Minneapolis: University of Minnesota Press, 1935), 179.
2. Chester G. Hearn, *Gray Raiders of the Sea* (Camden, Maine: International Marine Publishing, 1991), 83.
3. Edward Boykin, *Sea Devil of the Confederacy* (New York: Funk & Wagnalls, 1959), 188.
4. Ibid., 206.
5. Hearn, *Gray Raiders of the Sea*, 88.
6. Hill, *Sea Devils of the Sixties*, 184–85.
7. Howard K. Beale, ed., *Diary of Gideon Welles* (New York: W.W. Norton, 1960), I, 342–43.

8. Hill, *Sea Devils of the Sixties*, 185.
9. Welles, *Diary*, I, 380.
10. Charles Read to S.R. Mallory, Oct. 19, 1864, *Official Records (Navy)*, Series 1, II, 657.
11. Boykin, *Sea Devil of the Confederacy*, 218.
12. George W. Dalzell, *The Flight From the Flag* (Chapel Hill: University of North Carolina Press, 1940), 112.
13. Ibid., 83.

CHAPTER 11. The Representative Recruit for Abraham Lincoln
Adapted from an article first published in *Civil War Times Illustrated*, June 1978, and used by permission.

CHAPTER 12. The Fiery Trail of the *Alabama*
First published in *MHQ–Military History Quarterly*, Summer 1991, and used by permission.

CHAPTER 13. The Strange Fate of the CSS *Florida*
Published in *Civil War Times Illustrated*, in press 1997, and used by permission.
1. Hearn, *Gray Raiders of the Sea*, 54.
2. Boykin, *Sea Devil of the Confederacy*, 69.
3. Raphael Semmes, *Memoirs of Service Afloat* (Baton Rouge: Louisiana State University Press, 1996), 354–55.
4. Hearn, *Gray Raiders of the Sea*, 76–77.
5. John M. Taylor, *Confederate Raider: Raphael Semmes of the Alabama* (Washington, D.C.: Brassey's, 1994), 154.
6. Edward Boykin, *Ghost Ship of the Confederacy* (New York: Funk and Wagnalls, 1957), 297.
7. Hearn, *Gray Raiders of the Sea*, 98.
8. *ORN* Series I, vol. 2, 458–59.
9. Clarence E. Macartney, *Mr. Lincoln's Admirals* (New York: Funk & Wagnalls, 1956), 245–46.
10. Hearn, *Gray Raiders of the Sea*, 144.
11. Macartney, *Mr. Lincoln's Admirals*, 250.
12. Hearn, *Gray Raiders of the Sea*, 147.
13. *ORN* Series I, vol. 3, 276.
14. Ibid., 280.
15. Ibid., 285–87.
16. Ibid., 268.
17. Macartney, *Mr. Lincoln's Admirals*, 254–55.
18. Boykin, *Sea Devil of the Confederacy*, 290–91.

CHAPTER 14. Hancock the Superb
1. Glenn Tucker, *Hancock the Superb* (New York: Bobbs, Merrill, 1960), 150.
2. Almira R. Hancock, *Reminiscences of Winfield Scott Hancock* (New York: 1887), 66.
3. Tucker, *Hancock the Superb*, 97.
4. Hancock, *Reminiscences*, 94.
5. Tucker, *Hancock the Superb*, 246–47.
6. Ibid., 268.

7. Francis A. Walker, *General Hancock* (New York: 1894), 297–98.
8. Hancock, *Reminiscences*, 130.
9. David M. Jordan, *Winfield Scott Hancock* (Bloomington: Indiana University Press, 1996), 234.
10. Hancock to Sherman, June 8, 1881, Sherman Papers, Library of Congress.
11. Albert B. Paine, *Th: Nast, His Period and His Pictures* (Salem, N.H.: Ayer Co. Publishers, 1904), 438.
12. Taylor, *Garfield of Ohio*, 217.
13. Hancock, *Reminiscences*, 172.
14. Hancock to James R. Doolittle, Sept. 14, 1884, author's collection.
15. Hancock, *Reminiscences*, 240.
16. Charleston, South Carolina, *News and Courier*, quoted in Tucker, *Hancock*, 196.

CHAPTER 15. The Painter and the President
First published in *Civil War Times Illustrated*, February 1992, and used by permission.

CHAPTER 16. Folly at the Crater
Published in *MHQ* in press 1997, and used by permission.
1. Bruce Catton, *A Stillness at Appomattox* (Garden City, NY: Doubleday, 1963), 202.
2. Henry Pleasants Jr., *The Tragedy of the Crater*, 32.
3. William H. Powell, "The Battle of the Petersburg Crater," *Battles and Leaders of the Civil War*, IV, 545.
4. Ibid.
5. Douglas S. Freeman, *Lee's Lieutenants* (New York: Charles Scribner's Sons, 1944), III, 541.
6. Powell, "The Battle of the Petersburg Crater," 547.
7. Catton, *A Stillness at Appomattox*, 240.
8. Joseph J. Scroggs, "The Earth Shook and Quivered," *Civil War Times*, December 1972.
9. Powell, "The Battle of the Petersburg Crater," 551.
10. Catton, *A Stillness at Appomattox*, 243.
11. Ibid, 249.
12. Powell, "The Battle of the Petersburg Crater," 557.
13. Quoted in George S. Bernard, *War Talks of Confederate Veterans* (Dayton, Ohio: Morningside, 1981), 162.
14. Catton, *A Stillness at Appomattox*, 251.
15. J. Cutler Andrews, *The South Reports the Civil War*, 411.
16. *Official Records of the War of the Rebellion*, 40, Pt. I, p. 752.
17. U. S. Grant, *Memoirs*, II, 315.
18. Bernard, *War Talks*, 174.
19. Bruce Catton, *Grant Takes Command* (Boston: Little, Brown and Co., 1968), 325.
20. Charles S. Wainwright, "So Ends the Great Rebel Army," *American Heritage*, October 1962.

CHAPTER 17. The Man in the Gray Overcoat
1. Frederic Bancroft, *William H. Seward* (New York: Harper and Brothers, 1900), II, 418.
2. Frederick W. Seward, *Seward* (New York: Derby and Miller, 1891), III, 271.

3. Ibid., 271–72.
4. Benn Pitman, ed., *The Assassination of President Lincoln and the Trial of the Conspirators* (New York: Moore, Wilstach & Baldwin, 1865), 161.
5. Pitman, *The Assassination of President Lincoln*, 155.
6. Benjamin P. Thomas and Harold M. Hyman, *Stanton* (New York: Alfred A. Knopf, 1962), 396.
7. Patricia C. Johnson, *The Selected Diaries and Papers, 1858–1866, of Frances Adeline [Fanny] Seward*, Ph.D. diss., 2 vols. (processed), University of Rochester, 1964, vol. II, 890.
8. Pitman, *The Assassination of President Lincoln*, 157.
9. Johnson, "*Selected Diaries of Frances Adeline Seward*," vol. II, 891.
10. Taylor, *William Henry Seward*, 246.
11. Van Deusen, *William Henry Seward*, 414.
12. Taylor, *William Henry Seward*, 248.
13. George S. Bryan, *The Great American Myth* (New York: Carrick & Evans, 1940), 302–03.
14. Seward, *Seward*, III, 537–38.

CHAPTER 18. The Second Surrender
First published in *MHQ*, Spring 1991, and used with permission

CHAPTER 19

1. Semmes to Louisa Tremlett, Nov. 11, 1864, *Journal of Confederate History*, IV, 58–59.
2. Raphael Semmes, *Memoirs of Service Afloat During the War Between the States* (Baton Rouge: Louisiana State University Press, 1996), 794.
3. Ibid., 798.
4. J. Thomas Scharf, *History of the Confederate States Navy* (Baltimore: 1887), 746.
5. Burke Davis, *The Long Surrender* (New York: Random House, 1985), 34.
6. Taylor, *Confederate Raider*, 229.
7. Semmes Diary, *Alabama Review*, April 1975.
8. Taylor, *Confederate Raider*, 230.
9. Semmes, *Memoirs*, 819.
10. Semmes, *Diary*, April 16, 1865.
11. Taylor, *Confederate Raider*, 232.
12. Semmes, *Diary*, May 1, 1865.
13. Ibid., May 9, 1865.
14. Taylor, *Confederate Raider*, 242.

CHAPTER 20. "My God, You Cannot Iron Me!"

CHAPTER 21. Grover Cleveland and the Rebel Banners
First published in *Civil War Time Illustrated*, September/October 1993, and used by permission.

Index

Page numbers in *italics* indicate illustrations.

About the Author

JOHN M. TAYLOR graduated from Williams College in 1952 with honors in history, and earned a master's degree from George Washington University in 1954. From 1952 until 1987 he was employed by the U.S. government, in agencies concerned with intelligence and foreign affairs.

Mr. Taylor is the author of seven books in history and biography. His most recent biography, *Confederate Raider: Raphael Semmes of the Alabama*, was a 1995 selection of the History Book Club. His immediately previous work was another biography, *Williams Henry Seward: Lincoln's Right Hand*.

Mr. Taylor's earlier works include a biography of his father, *General Maxwell Taylor: The Sword and the Pen* (1989); a presidential biography, *Garfield of Ohio* (1970); and a book about presidential autographs, *From the White House Inkwell* (1968, rev. ed., 1989). He is a frequent contributor to historical magazines. He and his wife, Priscilla, live in McLean, Virginia.